LORD, TEACH US TO PRAY
A Guide to Christian Growth

LESLIE T. SEATON

Lord, Teach Us To Pray

Seaburn Publishing Group
P.O. Box 2085
LI, City NY 11102
www.seaburn.com

Cover designed by Lauren Lynch

ISBN 1-59232-063-5

Printed in the United States of America

LORD, TEACH US TO PRAY
A Guide to Christian Growth

LESLIE T. SEATON

TABLE OF CONTENTS

FOREWORD

In this book I have attempted to lead you through various episodes and experiences in Biblical History. It begins with the Advent, Christmas and New Year stories, proceeds through the Life and Teachings of Christ and His glorious Resurrection and Ascension. Then follows the Sections on Stewardship and Thanksgiving along with Home and Family life.

The book is not an anthology. It contains selections, prayers and meditations in conformity to the church year. The creative, prophetic, redemptive work is highlighted. Its main purpose is to bring salvation and strengthen your life as you travel the spiritual journey.

The selected passages are intended to strengthen your relationships in the home and family. Emphasis is given to the children and youth and their significance and importance to our society. One of the interesting features of this book is the Prayers of Children and Youth. Children are so often abused, mistreated, misguided; yet they are ex-pected to succeed and continue the generation. In order for this to happen, they must be nurtured.

The book ends with Our Mission and Message. Indeed we have a mission and message to the world. The fruit of the spirit is a fitting conclusion because we are called to be children and servants of God. As such we evidence changes in our lives.

It is the author's intention that change will take place in the reader's life. This should come about through prayer, meditation and a closer walk with God. These changes will manifest the Fruit of the Spirit. If we allow the Holy Spirit to lead our lives, there is no doubt that love, joy, peace, patience, kindness, goodness, faithfulness and gentle-ness, self-control, will enable us to become better citizens of this world and ultimately move on to be the inheritors of the New World of righteousness and peace.

L.S.

This book is dedicated to my wife
Harveybelle

ACKNOWLEDGEMENTS

I would like to acknowledge those persons who, through their dedication and unselfish commitment, have helped to bring this production to reality.

My wife Harveybelle Seaton, retired teacher and writer, for working assiduously on the draft; my daughter Alison Seaton, teacher at the Intermediate School New York, for reading the draft and making corrections; Veronica Pino, Associate Professor at Indian River Community College, for generously assisting in word processing; and Cindy Webster of Indian River Community College, for taking the manuscript to its completion.

To Lauren Lynch of Port St. Lucie for her graphic design of the cover of the book.

To Seaburn Publishing group of Long Island City, NY for bringing this publication to the reading public.

INTRODUCTION

Lord teach us to pray ...... *St. Luke 11:1*

Prayer is to entreat or petition. It is a supplication solemnly addressed to God. It is offered in the spirit of humility and is accompanied usually by adoration and confession, thanksgiving and supplication.

The Living Religions of the world place great emphasis on the spirituality of their adherents. An important aspect of this is prayer, meditation, and fasting. Those of us who are Christians have grown to appreciate prayer and its impact on our lives. Our Pastor/Priest, Elder, parents, and other individuals have prayed for us. Many of us have been nurtured through the prayer meetings of our church, and consequently, have placed a very high premium on prayer. We do this daily and can testify to the blessings we derive from praying to God our Father.

We are instructed by the Bible to pray for all classes and conditions of people, including rulers, kings, governors, presidents, and those who are placed to rule and govern us. We all need to nurture and develop our spirituality. Prayer is the key to that development.

In praying, we begin with God. We must know who He is, and have faith in Him before we can talk or communicate with Him. We know God through His revelation in Jesus Christ and the created order. To have faith in God is to have faith in Jesus Christ. But faith is not a magic word. Faith is belief in God, His Son Jesus Christ, and the teachings and doctrines of the Church. Through this kind of faith, we become "whole" persons. We receive healing and are restored to health. We are reconciled to God and our neighbors

and find peace with God. It is this peace with God that
results from communicating with Him through prayer
and meditation.

In early times, prayer was associated particu-
larly with sacrifice. Any place where sacrifice was
offered was a favorite place for prayer. Later the
Temple became the chief place where people went to
pray (Isaiah 56:7; Mark 11:17; Acts 3:1). The Jews
commonly prayed facing the Temple (1 Kings 8:30;
Psalms 5:7; Daniel 6:10-11). Notable prayers of the
Old Testament include the intercessions of Moses
(Numbers 14:13; Deut 9:26-29.), David's intercession
and Thanksgiving (2 Samuel 7:18-29), Solomon's
prayer for wisdom (1 Kings 3:6-9), Hezekiah's prayer
for and against Sennacherib (2 Kings 19:14-19),
Daniel's prayer for restoration of Jerusalem (Daniel
9:3-19). Several psalms are prayers (Psalm 17, 86, 90).

In the New Testament times, prayers were
offered in the Synagogues, on housetops, at street
corners and other outdoor places (Matthew 6:5, Acts
10:9, 16:13). Jesus made prayer an important subject in
His teaching. He taught that it should be sincere and
simple in form, It should be addressed to God as a
loving Father, It should be offered in the spirit of
brotherly unity, and should include a petition for the
welfare of enemies. (Matthew 5:44; 6:5-8; 7:7-11, 18-
19). He gave His disciples a model prayer(Matthew
6:9-13, Luke 11:1-4). It was His custom to pray pre-
ceding a great crisis. He prayed at his Baptism, at the
calling of the twelve, at the Transfiguration, the raising
of Lazarus, the Garden of Gethsemane and on the Cross
(Mark 14:32-39; Luke 6:12-13, 9:28-31, 23:34: John
11:41-44).

The Epistles of St. Paul are replete with exhorta-
tions to pray. There are biblical precedents for stand-

ing, sitting, kneeling, bowing and prostrating in praying (Genesis 24:26, 1 Samuel 1:26, 2 Samuel 7:18, 1 Kings 18:42, Luke 22:41).

In the Lord's Prayer or Model prayer, Jesus taught His disciples how to address God (Matthew 6:5-9). There are eight aspects to this Model Prayer. These are the Fatherhood of God, the nature of God, the Kingdom of God, the Will of God, God's providential love and sustenance, God's forgiveness of our sins, our forgiveness of each other, God's sustaining grace from temptation and deliverance from evil.

Prayer falls into the following categories: Adoration, Praise and Thanksgiving, Confession, Supplication and Intercession. When we follow these steps in praying, we will avoid vain repetitions. We will not heap up empty phrases in order to be heard for our many words, but in humility and faith we will address God and wait for the results. It may startle us to think that one addresses God. Yes, we speak to God in a personal way and He answers in a personal way according to our daily needs. Sometimes the answer is long in coming. We *may wait upon God* 'wait patiently for Him and He will give the desires of our hearts.' The result may either be positive or negative. We must accept His response.

My wife has always made her commendations for my prayers, and suggested that I write them for publication. This book is dedicated to her.

Prayers can be written or said extemporaneously or can exist in silence. I have tried to combine these methods in my ministry, whether in public or private. The following guideline indicates the method employed in this "exercise."
1.   An outline of that for which I need to pray.

2.   Rationalize on these by thinking philosophi-
      cally, theologically and emotionally (spiritually)
      in order to lead the individual, the family, and
      the congregation into prayer.

3.   Addressing God through the use of the outline,
      allowing the Holy Spirit to lead and direct my
      thinking. In so doing, head and heart are in
      conjunction (agreement) to the address that is
      made through His Son Jesus Christ for the
      edification of my hearers as well as my personal
      uplift. In this manner the Triune God, is ap-
      proached with the assurance that the utterances
      will be blessed by the Holy Spirit, and the
      hearers or myself will be spiritually enriched.

The Influence of Prayer on my Life.

      Many individuals have influenced my life
through prayer. They are: my father, Adolphus
Alexander Seaton (deceased). His prayers, especially
during a hurricane, resounded in our home. When he
prayed, he talked with God. His prayers offered his
family security and created a dependence on Divine
Providence. He caused us to feel secure in the midst of
the howling winds.

      Another important person was my minister, the
Reverend Daniel Emanuel Allen (deceased). His
prayers of intercession enabled his congregation and me
to reach out to the love of God in wonder and awe, for
God came near to us in worship.

      The Reverend Keith Tucker (deceased), Princi-
pal of Calabar Theological College, inspired me and the
other theological students as he addressed the transcendent Being and ushered us into His Presence. He
prayed to God in a personal way, even as one speaks to

a father and friend. Yet, there was dignity, majesty,
sincerity, humility, and eloquence in his prayers.

But what about my father-in-law, Hubert Shaw
(deceased)? He made a significant impact on me
through his prayers. The first time I met him in his
home, as well as the morning before my family and I
migrated to the United States, the prayers that were said
came from a man who knew how to talk with God. His
prayers were literally and theologically sound. They
were spiritually invigorating and inspiring.

The Increasing Value of Prayer

I have found the increasing value of prayer since
my conversion experience. This was personal. In my
preparation for examination, the literary work of John
Bunyan's Pilgrim's Progress greatly influenced my
decision to follow Christ. Those moments of contem-
plation in mind and soul brought me to the awareness of
the love of God for me, and the significance of the
Cross of Christ in my life. The result was a decision to
follow Christ through the waters of Baptism and church
membership.

My mother's death and approaching manhood
and life's career added another dimension to this dependence on God's mercy and love. It was during the dark
days of sadness and sorrow that I was thrown on God's
love to strengthen and guide me through pain and
suffering, and the successful completion on my examination.

The death of my father two weeks prior to my
first year final examination in Theological College
contributed much to my prayer life. I was faced with
the future without parents. I had saved my money from
a three-year teaching position. This was to enable me

to go through theological studies. After two years, this became exhausted. In all my endeavors in Seminary and other institutions of Higher Education, I have sought the Lord's guidance and He has sustained me with that Divine Providence.

Throughout my adolescent years and maturation, prayer became the key to my success. Personal talk with God has kept me in His Presence daily. It is a joy knowing that God always answers prayer. "The prayer of a righteous man has great power in its effects" (James 5:16)

I have grown to place a very high premium on prayer. Whether personal daily prayer, prayer for my family, prayer for my friends and the larger community at home and abroad, prayer for those in marriage, those on vacation, those facing life's challenges and their spiritual growth. The family altar on Sunday mornings is the place where the family and I share the blessings, hopes, aspirations, frustrations and problems of life.

I have tried to co-ordinate my education and expertise with prayer. This is unavoidable, when the intellectual approach is followed. I believe that communication reveals one's verbal advantage. The words we use tell who we are. Similarly in communicating with God, one ought to use the attributes with which one is endowed. As one represents Him or intercedes for the congregation, group or individual in a personal manner, one will communicate the language in which one is skilled or trained.

Whatever is the type of prayer, intellectual skills ought to be the banner under which God is addressed. But let me hasten to say this must not be the criterion for prayer. Intellectual skills will enable us to avoid the pitfall of vain repetitions. It must seek to be in tune

with the Spirit of God. Rationalism is no substitute for
"Enlightenment." The latter will come when we aspire
to be one with the Holy Spirit. This can occur any-
where, i.e. cathedral altar, sanctuary pew, the closet in
the home, the seat of a moving car or airplane, or even
in the quiet moments in the office, classroom, at the
desk, in the meadow, at the seaside, on top of the hill or
mountain, or in the open desert.

James Montgomery reminds us of the importance of prayer in these words:

"Prayer is the soul's
sincere desire, Uttered or
unexpressed
The notion of a hidden
fire
That trembles in the
breast.

Prayer is the burden of a
sigh,
The falling of a tear,
The upward glancing of
an eye,
When none but God is
near.

O Thou by whom we
come to God,
The life, the truth, the
way,
The path of prayer thyself
hath trod
Lord, teach us how to
pray."

I am therefore writing this book on prayer from my own vantage point as a Christian and one whose life has been changed through prayer. God is always coming to us. He prepares the way, directs our path in life, strengthens our faith in ourselves and in Him, and provides for us in ways in which we never dreamed.

I hope my readers will be inspired and strengthened as they read, and find comfort in these prayers. Each day is a journey with God. As you travel this pilgrimage, put your trust in God. He may be nearer to you than you think. Let Him be your guide and stay. The Psalmist encourages us to walk with God.

> "The Lord will keep you
> from all evil,
> He will keep your life.
> The Lord will keep your
> going out and your
> coming in
> From this time forth and
> for ever more." Psalm
> 121:7-8.

ADVENT TO CHRISTMAS

A Child is born, a son is given.

Scripture: *Isaiah 9:6-7*

> "To us a child is born, to us a son is
> given. And the government shall be
> upon his shoulder, and his name shall be
> called wonderful counselor, mighty God,
> everlasting Father, Prince of Peace. Of
> the increase of his government there will
> be no end."

Meditation

About five hundred years before the birth of
Jesus, the prophet Isaiah predicted that a child would be
born. He would be the deliverer of Israel. There are
two interpretations to this prediction. In the first in-
stance, the reference is to Cyrus the Great, under whose
reign the Jews were liberated from Babylon and returned to Jerusalem. The second interpretation is that
of the Christian Church wherein Jesus is seen as the
Messiah. This is characterized in the gospel presenta-
tions. Jesus' birth, life teachings, miracles, suffering,
death, resurrection, ascension and the establishment of
the church all refer to the role and functions of the Holy
child who became the Savior of the world. He is the
solution to all our problems. We need to open our
hearts to him and let him enter. He will change our
lives and be the Prince of Peace for us and for the
world.

Prayer

Our Father, accept our thanks for sending your
son into the world. He became our Saviour and Lord.
We thank you for Him as our counselor and guide,
shepherd, friend, Lord, Life, way, end. Help us to
commit our lives to Him, that not only at this Christmas
but throughout our lives we will celebrate the joy of
having found Christ and worship Him as your son and
our Lord. Amen.

Behold your God

Scripture: *Isaiah 40:9*

> "Jerusalem, herald of good tidings, says
> to the cities oh Judah, Behold your
> God."

Meditation

The prophet Isaiah addressed Israel with the
Messianic Hope. The day will come when God would
arise and His enemies would be scattered. Israel is to
take comfort that God would deliver her from the
Babylonian exile. This will eventually come to an end.
The glory of the Lord will be revealed and all flesh
shall see it together.

> "Every valley shall be lifted up and
> every mountain and hill made
> low. The uneven ground shall become
> level and the rough places a   plain. And
> the glory of the Lord shall be revealed."

When God comes, nations and peoples will take
comfort. He will feed His flock like a shepherd. He
will gather the lamb in His arms. He will carry them

in His bosom and gently lead those that are with young. Whether Babylon, Jerusalem or through the centuries or today, God is always there to comfort, to console, to bless, to cheer, to lead His people.

The Church is the herald of good tidings. Her message is to lift up Christ to the world. Two thousand years have not changed or eroded His appearance. The purpose for which Christ came is the same today as it was then and will be to the end of time. He came to redeem.

Whenever Christ is accepted, there is change and transformation. We need to accept Him into our lives. We need to realize that God is in control of the world and our lives.

Prayer

Eternal Father, creator and sustainer of the world, we praise you for your faithfulness to the world and all people. Help us to see the marvels of your grace in the Incarnation. Grant that Christ may be acknowl-edged and worshipped this Christmas and all times. God, you have been a comfort to the oppressed and enslaved. You have given them freedom and victory. Give us this day, the comfort we need, the peace of mind and the courage to follow you in order that we may herald your coming and the change that comes with believing on your power in the world. This we ask in the name of Christ our Lord. Amen.

Your Light has Come

<u>Scripture:</u> *Isaiah 60:1*

> "Arise, shine for your light has come.
> And the glory of the Lord has risen upon
> you."

<u>Meditation</u>

Light is an important phenomenon in nature, our daily lives and religion. It is indispensable to all living things. It is useful for growth, photosynthesis, productivity and economy. God is described as Light in all religions. The divine presence is referred to as the glory of the Lord. He is the Shekinah.

The pillar of cloud by day and the pillar of fire by night indicate God's presence in Israel in their earthly pilgrimage. The prophet Isaiah in the Messianic Hope illustrates God as the Light. He is the light that reveals His own glory. The psalmist says: "The Lord is my light and salvation, whom shall I fear. The Lord is the strength of my life, of whom shall I be afraid. The writer of the fourth gospel describes Jesus, as "the light that shines in the darkness, and the darkness has not overcome it." He is the true Light that enlightens every man coming into the world. Jesus speaks of Himself as the Light of the world, and any one who follows Him shall have the light of Life and shall not walk in darkness. We are called to be the Light of the world, a city that is set on a hill and cannot be hid.

The Hebrews commemorate their triumph over the Syrians in BC 165 by Judas Maccabaeus with the Great Feast of Lights—Hanukkah. The celebration lasts for eight days beginning December 2nd or a week before Christmas when eight candles are lit. The

Christian observes Advent, the coming of Christ in the
world, and lights the Advent Candles four Sundays
before Christmas, to signify the coming of Christ in the
world. The Nativity of Christ is celebrated with the
festival of Lights. Jesus is the eternal light that enlightens our daily path. Everyone who follows Him will not
walk in darkness but will have the light of life. We
must open our hearts to Him and walk in the light.

Prayer

> "Eternal light, eternal light,
> How pure the soul must be,
> When placed within thy searching sight,
> It shrinks not, but with calm delight,
> Can live and look on Thee."

Grant unto me, O God, the light of thy presence
this day, that I may live a victorious life and be of
service to those with whom I come in contact. Let the
world come to the knowledge of your saving grace and
accept you as the Great Light. Dispel darkness and
ignorance and bring us all to accept your love and
presence, through Jesus Christ who is the Light of the
world. Amen.

A Savior is Born

Scripture: *St. Luke 2:11*

> "To you is born this day in the city of David, a
> Savior who is Christ the Lord."

Meditation

The message of Christmas is: A Savior is born.
The prophesies of Isaiah and Micah were fulfilled in the

gospels. Isaiah states, "For to us a child is born, to us a son is given, and the government will be upon his shoulder and his name shall be called Wonderful Counselor, Mighty God, Everlasting Father, Prince of Peace. (Isaiah 9:6)

Micah records: "But you O Bethlehem Ephrathah, who are little to be among the clans of Israel, from you shall come forth one who is to be ruler in Israel, whose reign is from of old, from ancient days. (Micah 5:2)

The Christmas story is beautifully told by Luke in Chapter 2:8-11. The angelic chorus "Glory to God in the highest and on earth peace, goodwill to all men" brought awe and wonder to the shepherds. This has been the message of the centuries—A savior is born. Pilgrims from around the world gather in the church of the Nativity daily to worship and adore the Christ Child.

"O little town of Bethlehem, how still
we see Thee lie
Above the deep and dreamless sleep,
The silent stars go by.
Yet in the dark street shineth
The everlasting light
The hopes and fears of all the years
Are met in Thee tonight."

The first Christmas changed conditions for the humble, the poor, and the faithful. It brought hope to the poor and down-trodden, faith to those who were in expectancy. Courage to the weak and oppressed. It was a message of Peace and hope to the world. Even so it is to the world today. The world today is in trouble. The human condition needs God's love. We need the Savior's love. This will bring hope, courage, joy, peace and love to all people.

<u>Prayer</u>

Jesus, you are the Savior of the world. You are the center of my joy. Without you our lives are empty and world is bereft of love and peace. Grant O God, love to all of us that we may unite to herald you kingdom of righteousness and peace.

Accept O God, our thanks and praise for your gift to the world even Christ Jesus who came to save sinners. May He be born anew in our lives. May we be channels of blessings to our world and be enabled to serve you, the church, and our neighbors through the said Jesus, who is our Savior and Lord. Amen.

A Miracle of Love

<u>Scripture:</u> *St. John 1:14*

"The Word became flesh and dwelt among us, full of grace and truth. We beheld his glory, glory as of the only son from the Father."

<u>Meditation</u>

Word is power, speech, and communication. The history of Christian thought shows God as creative, prophetic, and revealed word. In creation He spoke and the word became the Act. Through the prophets the word became the utterance and in the Incarnation the word became deed—The word became flesh. This is a miracle. In the mystery of the incarnation, God took the initiative for our Salvation.

The idea of the Transcendent God is changed to that of the immanent God. God enters our existence, resides among us with the view of transforming our local habitat into a divine sanctuary. Throughout his life Jesus exemplified this. He was committed to the Redemption and Salvation of people. He communicates with the world by being in the world and suffering and dying for the world.

When individuals allow God to communicate with them, they discover that hostilities and tensions are removed, sickness and health is cured, alienation and separation is transformed to fellowship and communion with the triune God. Hatred and animosity is changed to love and peace. Life and death is like a beautiful symphony. This is the testimony of those who have found fellowship with the divine triad—Father, Son and Holy Spirit. May you find that fellowship.

Prayer

God and Father, Creator, Redeemer and Sustainer, accept our love and praise for the Redemption of the world by our Lord Jesus Christ. We thank you for the mystery and miracle of the Incarnation. We ponder that miracle and believe that you were and are in Christ redeeming the world. Accept our thanksgiving for salvation we receive by believing on the miracle of his birth, his death and resurrection. Give us the reassurance that He is in the world and calling us to be His disciples and emissaries of the kingdom. Save us from sinfulness and create a clean heart and a right spirit in us that we may serve you in holiness and righteousness all our days through Jesus Christ our Lord. Amen.

NEW YEAR

Forgetting the past; Reaching for the future.

Scripture: *Philippians 3:13-14*

> "Brethren, I do not consider that I have
> made it my own, but one thing I do,
> forgetting what lies behind, straining
> forward to what lies ahead, I press on
> toward the goal for the prize of the
> upward call of God in Christ Jesus."

Meditation

St. Paul in his writing to the Church at Philippi
emphasized the change that took place in his life by
Jesus Christ. He persecuted the church especially going
to Damascus to arrest the Christians. But his life was
changed by Christ. He was called to be an apostle to
the Gentiles. In his ministry he also suffered persecution. Yet in his quest for the prize he had to set his goal
and forget the inglorious past. This was to attain the
imperishable crown or the prize of the "upward call of
God in Christ Jesus."

We are called to reach out for this prize. We
need to discipline ourselves like the Olympic runner
and win the prize at the end of life's journey. Like St.
Paul we all have the inglorious past, but let us not look
back, let us look forward with faith in Christ and we
will win the race.

Prayer

God our father, Father of our Lord Jesus Christ,
accept our thanks for sending Jesus into the world, and

for all who like St. Paul have run the Christian race with satisfaction and joy, and have entered their rest. Inspire us by your spirit and word that we may forget the sinful past and with faith in you and our Lord Jesus Christ, run the race that is set before us, looking to Him who is the author and finisher of our faith. Be our guide this day and always. This we ask in the name of Jesus Christ. Amen.

Change

Scripture: *Revelation 21:1-7*

> "Then I saw a new heaven and a new earth, for the first heaven and the first earth had passed away ...He who sat upon the throne said: Behold I make all things new ...I am the Alpha and Omega, the beginning and the end...I will be his God and he shall be my son."

Meditation

Change is any variation or alteration in form, state, quality or essence. It is the passing from one state, form or place, to another. It is also a succession of one thing in place of another. This metamorphosis takes place in form, structure, appearance, character or circumstance. There are various changes that occur in time. Examples of these are cosmic changes in which the world becomes larger or smaller by means of discoveries and inventions.

Chemical and biological changes in the natural and human world and scientific discoveries have attempted to conquer outer space and explain the mystery of Mars. Population and demographic changes have changed the rural into urban environment whilst the metropolis has replaced the village. Cultural and aesthetic changes have advanced human developments. Education and learning have removed ignorance and illiteracy into higher education and research. Such enlightenment has created professions and vocations as well as developing the skills to create an educated and industrialized society. Such advantages have given rise to an economic boom.

But there are moral and spiritual changes that affect us. Life is built on moral principles. The ethics of our society condemns evil and uphold the good, showing that the virtues do not change. Truth is truth in any part of the world. Spirituality is born of religion and religion is a phenomenon that confronts humanity from the beginning of time.

All religion has its spirituality. The Christian religion highlights the spirituality in God's revelation through His son Jesus the Christ. It is this Christocentrism that the author of the book of Revelation highlights when he writes: "He who sat upon the throne said, 'Behold I make all things New. . .I am the Alpha and the Omega, the beginning and the end." Those of us who accept Him as our personal Savior will experience this change. All things will become new in our lives. This is the change that is above all changes.

Prayer

Eternal God and Father of the human race, accept our thanks and gratitude for your steadfastness to all throughout the age. We thank you that there is no change or
variableness in your nature and love. Grant unto us O Lord, a clearer perception of your Revelation in history and in Jesus Christ, in order that we may discern more

fully your goodness for all people and us.

Let your blessing be upon us this day as we work to establish love, justice and peace in our society. We pray for change in our attitudes and interactions with those in home, factory, office, industry, trade commerce, politics and government, agriculture, and above all the church, in order that we may all labor for the building of your kingdom on earth. Help us to acknowledge you as the Alpha and Omega of our lives and work, through Jesus Christ our Lord. Amen.

All Things New

Scripture: *Revelation 21:5-6*

> And he who sat upon the throne said "Behold, I make all things new.' Also he said, "Write this, for these words are trustworthy and true." And he said to me "It is done. I am Alpha and Omega, the beginning and the end. To the thirty, I will give from the fountain of the waters of life without payment."

Meditation

The book of Revelation is called the Apoca-lypse. It is futuristic and envisages the change from the old to the new. The writer of this book looked forward to the day when the "old Jerusalem" would change to the "New Jerusalem." Indeed the city of God would be established forever. We are called to enlist in this spiritual kingdom. We must allow God to be the beginning and the end of our Christian journey. God must be the Alpha and the Omega in our lives. Let us therefore pursue our Christian journey with Him as our guide.

Prayer

God, our Father and Redeemer, we thank you for your permanence in the world and in our lives. From the beginning you are God, today you are our God, and will be forever. Grant that in the changing scenes of life we may perceive your steadfast love and be led to glorify your name. Help us to know that you are the Alpha and Omega—the beginning and the end and that we may rest assured that you will guide us today and forever. Amen.

A New Beginning

Scripture: *Philippians 3:7-9, 13-14*

> "But whatever gain I had, I counted a loss for the sake of Christ. Indeed I count everything a loss because of the surpassing worth of knowing Christ Jesus my Lord. For this sake I have suffered the loss of all things, and count them as refuse in order that I may gain Christ . . . Brethren, I do not consider that I have made it may own. But one thing I do, forgetting what lies behind and straining forward to what lies ahead, I press on toward the goal for the prize of the upward call in God in Christ Jesus."

Meditation

St. Paul in his letter to the Church in Philippi emphasized the past, present and future in his life. His goal is to have Christ in his life. A persecutor of the Christians, he met Jesus on the Damascus road. His life was changed. He became the Apostle to the Gentiles and wrote most of the Epistles in the New Testament. In these, he expressed his theology, the doctrines of the church and the affirmation of the church's faith. As a learned scholar, a Jew, a Pharisee, he had a rich heritage but these he counted loss for the excellency of Christ Jesus. His aim was "to press toward the goal for the prize of the upward call of God in Christ Jesus."

The Philippian jailer was converted and the church was established at Philippi by Paul. The grace of God is available to us. This will enable us to attain to the imperishable crown in Christ Jesus our Lord and those things we hold dear unto ourselves, will fade away or be counted as loss, for the surpassing worth of knowing Christ.

Prayer

Lord Jesus, I come to you renouncing the evils of my past. In this act of confession, forgive me and renew a right spirit in me. Like St. Paul, I crave the excellency of Christ Jesus my Lord. Pour thy blessing on me this day. Inspire me by thy word and spirit. Challenge me to go forward in faith for in doing so I will attain the crown of righteousness. Let me dedicate myself for service, whether at home, work, church or community. This I ask in your name. Amen.

Baptism

Scripture: *Matthew 3:13-17*

"Then Jesus came from Galilee to the Jordan to John to be baptized of him. . . Let it be so now, for thus it is fitting for us to fulfill all righteousness. . .This is my beloved Son with whom I am well pleased."

Meditation

Baptism is an ancient rite for cleansing and initiation into the cults or into a religion. John the Baptist was preparing the Jewish community for the reception of the Messiah who would baptize them with the Holy Spirit. To be included in the Messianic plan they were to repent. Jesus requested baptism from John the Baptist. John indicated that he had no need to be baptized since he was the Messiah. But Jesus' request was granted. He was acknowledged by God to be His Son in whom He is well pleased.

The Greek word for Baptism is to immerse or to be plunged under water or be buried. St. Paul writing to the Church in Rome told them "we are buried therefore with Him by baptism unto death so that as Christ was raised from the dead through the glory of the Father we too might walk in newness of life."

Two modes of baptism are stated in the New Testament. Baptism by water on the faith of the believer and baptism by the Holy Spirit. The Church has practiced both. But the overriding factor is the Holy Spirit. Our baptism "separates" us from the world and unites us in the body of Christ. All who are baptized are one in Christ. Are you a part of the body of Christ? Have you been baptized by the Holy Spirit?

Prayer

God, our Father, we thank you for our Baptism which unites us in the body of Christ. You have caused your Holy Spirit to fill our lives. Accept our praise for the ways in which your spirit has controlled our daily living. We pray for this constant baptism in your church. Grant that all who believe may become mes-sengers of your grace and love in order that your re-demptive love may be experienced throughout the world. This we pray in the name of Jesus Christ our Lord. Amen.

HIS TEACHING MINISTRY

Blessed Are You

Scripture: *St. Matthew 5:2-11*

> "Blessed are the poor in spirit, for theirs is the kingdom of God...and persecute you and utter all kinds of evil against you falsely on my account."

Meditation

The world's living religions have their teachings or rules that govern the conduct of their followers. Christianity, unlike other religions, is a religion of faith and not one of rules and forms. However, in the New Testament there are certain precepts that guide Christian conduct. In Matthew the sayings or teachings of Jesus to His disciples are put together in what is generally known as the Sermon on the Mount. In this Jesus describes the conduct of the members of the new kingdom of righteousness "Blessed are the poor in Spirit for theirs is the kingdom of heaven . . .Rejoice and be glad, for your reward is great in heaven for so men persecuted the prophets who were before you."

There are nine Beatitudes or Blesseds, and each has its assurance. The disciples are not only asked to attain righteousness in the Kingdom, they are given the assurance of present satisfaction and joy. They will be comforted, they shall inherit the earth, they shall be satisfied, they shall obtain mercy, they shall see God, they shall inherit the kingdom of God, they shall rejoice and be glad, for as prophets they will be persecuted, but their reward will be great in heaven.

With this new ethic, they are to change the world and be instruments in a new reign or righteousness. The righteousness has as its core the message of Redemption, reconciliation, forgiveness and love. This is what the world, the church and each one of us needs if we are to survive and be the children of God.

<u>Prayer</u>

O Lord our God, how excellent is your name in all the earth! We thank you for the way of righteousness. You are right and just. Your son Jesus Christ has shown us the way of righteousness. In His teachings he has called us to a new ethic. Help us to find that path and walk in it. We pray for mercy, for comfort, for peace, for righteousness, for meekness and purity of heart. We know that in our quest for you we will find peace. Help us to walk close to you and lead the world in love. Your son is our Lord and Savior. He endured the cross and became the victor over death and the grave. In his risen power, He calls us to follow Him this day. May we lead others to your kingdom and be instruments of righteousness to our world, through Jesus Christ our Lord. Amen.

Two Indispensables to Christian Discipleship

<u>Scripture: *St. Matthew 5:13-16*</u>

"You are the salt of the earth...you are the light of the world...Let your light so shine before men, that they may see your good works and give glory to your Father who is in Heaven."

<u>Meditation</u>

In the Sermon on the Mount, Jesus explained to

His disciples the rudiments of the New Ethic. With
every blessing in the Beatitudes comes a promise in the
New Kingdom. With persecution comes the assurance
that great will be the reward in heaven and the comfort
that the Disciples are not the first to be persecuted. For
"so persecuted they the prophets which were before
you."

Jesus selected two everyday necessities to be the
guiding light to discipleship. They are the indispens-
ables of life. These are salt and light. Salt has a curative value. It heals, it cures. Salt preserves. Salt offers
taste and makes our diet palatable. The Christian
Disciple is to offer curative, preservative, healing value
to the world. His/her act of love is indispensable to the
world. He/she cannot be insipid.

Light is energy. Light dispels darkness. All life
seems to depend upon light. It is the means of production. It sustains plants and animals. One of the basic
principle in germination is the fact that the seed needs
warmth in order to germinate. That warmth is energy
from the sun. Christians, under the Holy Spirit form the
source of energy to the world. They are the means of
dispelling the darkness that causes man to grope in sin.
They are to illumine the path in the world in order that
weary pilgrims can travel with safety. The divine
source of energy is given by Jesus to the Christian to
aid the weary traveler on his journey.

We cannot lose the salt in us nor can we allow
the light in us to be extinguished. "Let your light so
shine before men, that they may see your good works
and give glory to your Father who is in heaven."

<u>Prayer</u>

Jesus, you are the light of the world. You have called us to be your lights in this world of ignorance and sin. You have called us to be the salt of the earth. Enable us by your spirit to give flavor to our society in order that righteousness and peace will prevail. May the salt and light in us be ever effective and each individual will be changed for your service. Grant that our actions and deeds may enhance your kingdom. Bless all Christians in their witness and endeavors to extend your kingdom. Keep them (us) steadfast in the faith. So may we live and anticipate the kingdom when righteousness shall cover this land, as the waters cover the ocean depths. Amen

Called to be perfect

<u>Scripture:</u> *St. Matthew 5:48*

"You therefore must be perfect as your heavenly father is perfect."
<u>Mediation</u>

The call to be perfect which was made by Jesus to His disciples is a tall order. To be perfect is to be without fault, without flaw, without blemish, without error, or mistakes. It is humanly impossible.

Perfection implies standards, order, discipline, and impeccability. There is no perfect human being. There are however, outstanding professionals and administrations. Some of us, according to our training and discipline are more perfect than others. There is some order and decorum about and around us. Our manner of speech, our manner of dress, our deportment, our politeness, all reveal perfection. Some of us are

sloppy; others are rigid and follow routines. Still there
are those who act according to the situation that arises.

The call to discipleship is not mechanistic. It is
not a proficiency call. It is a call to be engrossed in the
grace of God. It is a call to piety, to saintliness. This
saintliness is the standard or measurement for our daily
living. It is in this respect that we fall short.

The Disciples are called to be like God. Is this
possible? That impeccability to which we are called
seems highly impossible when human standards or
measurement are applied. We all fall short. But, by the
grace of God, we can attain to this perfection.

Saintliness is a call to utter dependence on the
grace of God for our support in daily living and human
encounters and interactions. Whatever we do is justified
by God. Herein lies our perfection. We need to let Him
control our lives and use us in changing the world.

Prayer

Lord Jesus, you have called us to perfect even as
the Father is perfect. We are weak and incapable of
achieving this. Only by your grace can we live and
serve in this world. Grant O Lord to me this day that
portion of your grace that will enable me to praise you,
serve you, at home, work, community, and the nation. I
do not ask to be the perfect person, but only to be of
service to someone in need, so that my living will not
be in vain. Amen.

Forgive Our Debts

Scripture: _Matthew 6:12_

> "And forgive us our debts, As we for-
give our debtors."

Meditation

Jesus taught his disciples that forgiveness
should be an integral part of their prayers and living.
We are all debtors. We have transgressed God's laws
and need to be forgiven. As fallible beings we fall short
of the requirement of God. In so many ways we have
sinned against God. If we are to be right with God then
we need to be forgiven.

Forgiveness implies repentance or godly sorrow
for our sins. It calls for confession. In order to confess
our guilt one needs to express godly sorrow or contrition for one's past deeds or actions. In confessing our
sins to God We pray for forgiveness and healing.

But forgiveness also requires an
acknowledgement of the wrong done to the individual.
It is conditional. We are to forgive one another. If you
forgive men their trespasses, your heavenly Father also
will forgive you. But if you do not forgive men their
trespasses, neither will your Father forgive your trespasses. The state of mind is of great importance. One
should not expect God's forgiveness if one cannot
forgive.

Shakespeare's expression "To err is human, to
forgive is divine" is applicable to each one of us. As
finite beings we are all in this predicament of erring.
We all need to be forgiven. Such forgiveness comes
directly from our sinfulness, and because of our sinful-

ness we cause pain on our neighbors. In our weakness
we need the mercy and forgiving love of God in order
that we can have peace with God and peace with our
neighbors.

What about our relationships with spouse,
children, other relatives, co-workers, friends, and
neighbors? How often do we forgive them? It may not
be seventy times seven, but as often as the need arises.
We are to forgive one another, even as we are forgiven
by God. God, in Jesus Christ has forgiven us. Jesus
prayed for his enemies while on the cross "Father,
forgive them for they do not know what they are doing."

<u>Prayer</u>

Our Father and our God, we thank you for your
love in the creation and redemption of the world. In
Jesus Christ you have become real to us. We thank you
for His life, teachings, miracles, suffering, death, and
resurrection. He has taught us how to love and how to
die. Enable us in our daily pursuits to acknowledge
your forgiveness of our sins and to forgive those who
trespass against us. May we rise above the petty jealousies that would mar our spiritual union with our neighbors and with you. May we strive for peace with you
and with those with whom we come in contact. Grant,
O Lord, forgiveness to us this day and so may we ever
love and serve you through Jesus Christ our Lord.
Amen.

Do not be anxious about tomorrow

Scripture: *St. Matthew 6:34*

> "Therefore do not be anxious about tomorrow, for tomorrow will be anxious for itself. Let the days own trouble be sufficient for the day."

Meditation

We live in a world of competition. Every facet of life requires some planning. Farmers, entrepreneurs, co-operations, military, government, education, churches, parents, scientists, and a host of other groups and individuals make plans for the future. We are concerned about the future and what it will bring. Such concern can develop into anxiety. Anxiety can be a good thing and it can be bad. It can lead to greater productivity and it can lead to frustration, schizophrenia, and paranoia.

Jesus taught His disciples how to avoid anxiety that would lead to the latter of these suggested thoughts. They must put their trust in God's providential care. To Him, life is more than food, and the body more than raiment. The birds of the air, man's physical growth, the lilies of the field surpassed the beauty of Solomon's glory. God clothes the grass in the field. He supplies food for man and beast.

"Therefore do not be anxious saying…What shall we drink or what shall we wear? Your heavenly Father knows what you need. Seek first his kingdom and his righteousness and all these things shall be yours as well."

This is a timely reminder for all of us. In a

world of material wealth and luxury we tend to want more and become anxious for what is not. We need to learn to be content with the blessings of God, to trust Him for His goodness, and to count our blessings, naming them one by one. It will surprise us what the Lord has done in our lives.

Prayer

God, you have provided all things for our comfort and human development. We thank you for the abundance of natural resources that make life meaningful for us. We thank you for human resources with which our world is endowed. Grant that we may use these resources for our enrichment and in grateful acknowledgement of your love in creation. Rid our minds of anxiety that leads to futility and not creativity. Enable us to count our blessings and seek your love. May your kingdom come in our lives, even as it is in heaven. Let your blessings be upon commerce, industry, business, education, government, home, family, and every individual in our world. May we all trust your love and care. This we ask in the name of Jesus, our Teacher and Lord. Amen.

New wine needs new bottles

Scripture: *Matthew 9:17*

"Neither is new wine put into old wineskins. If it is, the skin burst, and the wine is spilled, and the skins are destroyed. But new wine is put into fresh wineskins, and so both are preserved."

Meditation

It is amazing how in his teachings Jesus utilized the ordinary and mundane. Out of these he illustrated something of the meaning of life. The parable, the Sermon on the Mount, the new and old cloth, new and old wineskins are examples of his skill in the use of the little things to objectify great truths. The old wineskin bottles are not durable for unfermented grape juice. When fermentation takes place the contents will rent the wineskins. If both bottle and wine are to be of any value, then new grape juice must be put in new bottles. Such containers will have a futuristic purpose.

Similarly, the new birth in the life of an individual requires a new wineskin. The principle of regeneration requires a new man in Christ Jesus. We must give up the old. Forsake the old paths and turn to new ways of loving. It is dangerous to think that the converted can still live in the old frame. There must be new wineskins and new cloth. One cannot put on a new patch on the old garment. It is not aesthetic, neither is it durable. When it shrinks, there may be a greater rent than before. Consequently, the new person in Christ must be changed. Metamorphosis must take place and a new life must emerge. This new life is what believing in Christ offers to all who call on His name. What about you?

Prayer

O Lord, we thank you for the newness and richness of your love for us. Each day brings us new and rich blessings. We thank you for the change that comes to us in believing on your work of grace for us. Sustain us this day by your amazing grace. Lord, we thank you for your teachings. Help us to understand the meaning of the new and old garment, the new and old wineskins.

Through these practical teachings, may we see the changes in our faith and renewal. May the richness of your spirit sustain us in these days of stress and strain. May we be filled with the new wine that is supplied by your grace and love. May we be the channels through which this is mediated to those with whom we come in contact in home, family, workplace, church, and the world. This we ask in Jesus' name. Amen.

Privilege brings responsibility

Scripture: *St. Matthew 19:21*

> "Jesus said to him 'If you would be perfect, go, sell what you possess and give to the poor, and you will have treasure in heaven; and come, follow Me'."

Meditation

Many of us are called to specific tasks, professions, vocations, missions, and works of charity. Some of these calls take us from obscurity to celebrity and the hall of fame. Indeed this is the path from which the leaders of the world have traveled. We become privileged. With this privilege, comes responsibility.

This theological idea runs throughout the pages of Holy writ. The Old Testament portrays Israel as the chosen of God. In such choice, Israel had proven to be responsible and had a message and mission to the ancient world. In the New Testament, the New Israel is chosen by God to bear His name to the gentiles and the kings of the earth. Such a gospel spells a new dispensation for the people of God. We are called by God. We become a chosen people and we are to change the world by our life and witness.

The rich young ruler (sometimes called lawyer) wanted to know from Jesus what good deed he should do to inherit eternal life. Both Teacher and student knew the law, but the student was deficient. He had kept the law from his youth, "What do I still lack?", he asked. Jesus' reply defied his impeccability. You hold onto your material wealth too much. Go, sell your possessions, give something to the poor (charity). You will have treasure in heaven. Come, identify with me. Learn of my sorrow and suffering as well as my joy and victory. You will be richly blessed.

Is this not what we are called to do today? Identify with Christ. This is a call to serve. Be responsible for your world and it will be a better place because you cared.

Prayer (The prayer of St. Francis)

> Lord, make me a channel of thy peace
> That where there is hatred, I may bring love
> That where there is wrong, I may bring the spirit of forgiveness
> That where there is despair, I may bring hope
> That where there is error, I may bring truth
> That where there is discord, I may bring harmony
> That where there are shadows, I may bring light
> That where there is sadness, I may bring joy
> Lord, grant that I may seek to comfort,

rather than to be comforted
To understand, rather than to be under-
stood
To love, rather than to be loved, for it is
in giving that one receives
It is in self-forgetting that one finds
It is by forgiving that one is forgiven
It is by dying that one awakens to Eter-
nal life.

He was Transfigured

Scripture: *St. Mark 9:2-8*

"After six days, Jesus took with Him,
Peter and James and John, and led them
up a high mountain apart by themselves,
and He was transfigured before
them…And a cloud overshadowed them,
and a voice came out of the cloud: 'This
is my beloved Son, listen to him.' And
suddenly looking around they no longer
saw anyone with them but Jesus only."

Meditation

The Transfiguration is beyond our comprehen-
sion. Mountain, cloud, theophanies, spirits, and voice
are not unfamiliar to religion. God has spoken through
these phenomena before, but this is the first time that
the Disciples saw Jesus so luminous. Did this scare or
terrify them? Did the appearance of Moses and Elijah
astound them? Moses and Elijah represented the law
and the prophets. The interpretation for their presence
suggests that in Jesus the law and the prophets were
fulfilled.

Tabernacles were to erected as temporary abode
for the three, but in a moment, only Jesus remained
with them. He was affirmed by God to be the beloved
Son. The disciples and future believers were to respond
to Him. We need to see Christ in all His glory and
respond by opening our hearts to him this day and
always. We too shall be changed.

Prayer

Dear God, I thank you for sending Jesus to be
my Savior and Redeemer. I thank you for His mountain
top experience and your confirmation of His Sonship
and Lordship. Help me in my belief to accept Him in all
His glory. Save me from making external tabernacles.
By your redeeming grace, help me to open my heart to
Him and worship Him as my Savior and Lord. Grant
that I may be of service to someone today, through
Jesus Christ my Lord. Amen.

Give Us Salvation

Scripture: *St. Mark 11:9-10*

"Hosanna! Blessed be he who comes in
the name of the Lord. Blessed be the
kingdom of our David that is coming.
Hosanna in the highest!"

Meditation

There is a common agreement in the gospels
that Jesus' last visit to Jerusalem occurred a few days
before the Passover. At that time, pilgrims from far and
near were gathering in Jerusalem to commemorate the
redemption of Israel from Egyptian bondage, and to re-
enact the Passover. The entry of Jesus was unusual.
His actions became acted parables.

St. Mark declared, "When they drew near to
Jerusalem to Bethphage and Bethany, at the Mount of
Olives, he sent out two of his disciples with the instruction to go into the village opposite them, where they
would find a colt on which no man ever sat. They were
to untie the colt and bring him. If any man asked them
why they where doing this, they were to reply that the
Lord needed the colt and would send it back immediately."

The colt was brought to Jesus. He threw his
garment on it and sat upon it. Many spread their garments on the road; others spread leafy branches. They
tore down branches of trees and strew them in the way,
those who went before and who followed called out
"Hosanna! Blessed be the kingdom of our father
David." The prophecy of Zechariah was fulfilled,
"Rejoice greatly, O Daughter of Zion! Shout O Daughter of Jerusalem! Lo, your king comes to you triumphant and victorious, humble and riding on an ass, on a
colt, the foal of an ass." (Zechariah 9:9)

The Christian Church observes this episode in
the life of Jesus as Palm Sunday. Palm Sunday is to
herald Salvation. This is the positive side to the drama
of salvation.
Although it leads to tragedy and death on the cross, we
must remember that the triumphant entry introduced the
holiest week in the Christian year. It led to Gethsemane
and Golgotha. For this reason, Jesus could not avoid
Jerusalem. In fact, he never came out the same Jesus.
Herein lies our salvation – indeed the salvation of the
world. The cry for salvation is an individual cry, as well
as a cosmic cry. We all need salvation. It's the unend-
ing cry from all who are in need, whatever that need
may be. But above all, it is the cry for salvation from
sin.

Prayer

Lord Jesus, Savior of the world, my Savior and friend, accept the praise I offer you this day for your salvation to the world. I thank you that I am one for whom you gave your life. I thank you for the message of the gospel in every age proclaiming the good news of salvation to all people. Bless us with your spirit. Cleanse us from every sin. Strengthen us with your grace so that in our endeavors we may be triumphant in our witness and bring others to your salvation, O Lord Jesus, save us now, we beseech Thee. Amen.

They also serve

Scripture: *St. Mark 14 : 9*

> "And truly, I say to you, whenever the gospel is preached in the whole world, what she has done will be told in memory of her."

Meditation

Women have had significant impact on history and culture. They have fulfilled the roles of queens, rulers, leaders, heroines, prophetesses, teachers, counselors, and mothers. In the contemporary world, the list of their achievements extends to include scientists and astronauts. This is not a liberation of the species or gender but a fulfillment of their God-given endowment.

But women are known for their emotion and sentimentality. They are good entertainers and make their male counterparts feel good at home and in the public arena. In this incident described by Mark, Jesus is knocked off his feet, when in the house of Simon the

leper, an unnamed woman opened a flask of pure nard
and poured it over his head. The incident is also recorded as taking place in Bethany. Suggestions are that
this woman could be Mary, the sister of Lazarus of
Bethany, or perhaps, Mary of Magdala from whom
Jesus had rebuked the devil. The latter could be associated with her intention to express gratitude for her
liberation from sin. Many criticized her action and
regarded it as waste. Jesus regarded this as a beautiful
act. She had anointed him for his burial and wherever
the gospel is preached in the whole world, what she has
done will be told in memory of her.

History has recorded the actions of women in
the fields of religion, politics, art, science, education,
government, social services, health, and civic leadership; but more so in the home and family. Women
today must continue their leadership in these areas and
effect the changes that will create a new world for
people. What role do you play in society today?

Prayer

God, you have created male and female and
placed them in the world to replenish the earth. We
thank you for women whose role extends beyond
procreation. You have endowed women with many and
varied attributes and have led them in paths of leadership over the centuries. Accept our gratitude for the
beauty in the leadership of women in home, society,
and the world. Bless all women who lead in these areas.
We thank you for the gospel – the good news that has
come from the leadership of women around the world.
May their leadership inspire the young to be courageous
in the midst of hardships and difficulties and accept the
leadership that is necessary and important in the transformation of our contemporary world. This we ask for
the sake of all women and in the name of Jesus Christ

our Lord. Amen

The Last Supper

Scripture: *St. Mark 14: 22-24*

> "As they where eating, He took bread
> and blessed and broke it and gave it to
> them and said, 'Take, this is my body.'
> And He took the cup and when He had
> given thanks, He gave it to them and
> they all drank of it. And He said to them,
> 'This is my blood of the covenant which
> is poured out for many.'"

Meditation

The Passover was the Last meal Jesus had with His disciples before his crucifixion. Some scholars say that it bears resemblance to the Kiddush, which was a consecration or mealtime ritual of sanctification of the feast days. Others say it was like a Jewish fellowship meal.

In the supper, Jesus distributed bread, which represented His body, and wine, which represented His blood. It promised the disciples a share in the eschatological kingdom by which is made possible, His death. The past, present, and future is represented in the New Covenant established by Christ.

Throughout the centuries, the Christian community has celebrated this feast (supper). It is a perpetual remembrance of the sacrifice of Jesus Christ for the world. It is a bond and pledge of our communion with Christ and with each other as members of Christ's body.

Prayer

Lamb of God that takes away the sin of the world, have mercy upon me. Holy and Righteous God, accept my thanks and praise for this sacrament which you have given in your son Christ Jesus who became my sacrifice. Cleanse me from every sin and sustain me with your grace. Grant that this Holy Communion may bring me closer to you and my Savior Jesus Christ. Help me to seek you in the breaking of bread and the drinking of the cup through Jesus Christ my Lord. Amen.

Gethsemane

Scripture: *St. Mark 14: 32-42*

> "And they went to a place which was called Gethsemane. And he said to his disciples, 'Sit here while I pray….Rise, let us be going, see the betrayer is at hand.'"

Meditation

The last evening in the life of Jesus was terrible. His soul became very sorrowful, even to death. The cup of bitterness loomed heavily on him. He prayed to the father, "All things are possible to Thee, remove this cup from me, yet not what I will, but what you will." He prayed alone, leaving him to wrestle alone with the approaching anguish of the cross. He realized that the hour had come and like a stoic, he advised the Disciples to "Rise, let us be going, my betrayer is at hand."

There has never been such anguish, sorrow, and pain, yet Jesus bore it all. He knew that it was for this purpose he came into the world. He would accomplish his objective and would change Gethsemane, the garden of sorrow, into the Garden of Victory, even the Resurrection.

We too, have our Gethsemane and we too, can have our Resurrection by believing in His risen power – "Rise, let us be going" is the clarion call to discipleship. Sorrow and defeat will give way to joy and victory in Jesus Christ. This comes by believing on Him. Do you believe He can change your sorrow and suffering into joy and gladness?

Prayer

O, Lamb of God who takes away the sin of the world, look in tender mercy on us and change our sorrow into joy. You have overcome Gethsemane and the cross. Your resurrection has brought light and life to the world. Strengthen our faith and illumine our path in order that we may have victory in your name and for your sake we pray this prayer, O Lord. Amen.

The Physical and Spiritual Birth

Scripture: *St. John 3: 6-7*

> "That which is born flesh is flesh, and that which is born spirit is spirit. Do not marvel that I said to you 'you must be born anew.'"

Meditation

Most of us are familiar with the story of Nicodemus and Jesus. If you are not, here it is in a nutshell.

Nicodemus, a rabbi and teacher of the law went to Jesus to appraise his knowledge. Instead of a dialectic discourse on the law, Jesus confronted Nicodemus with the New Birth. This baffled his mind. How could this be when he is old? Such misconception of the New Birth did not startle Jesus. Instead, he drew a lesson from the wind. It goes, it comes, one hears the sound, but cannot tell its direction, even so is the one that is born from above. There is a difference between the physical and spiritual world. That which is born of the flesh is flesh and that which is born of the spirit is spirit. The spiritual birth takes place when one believes on the Son of God. One is endowed with the gift of Eternal life and will not perish. The cardinal thing in such experience is "God so loved the world that He gave his only son that whosoever believes in him should not perish but have eternal life." (John 3:16) Do you believe this? Do you have life in Jesus Christ?

Prayer

Eternal God, creator and sustainer, from everlasting to everlasting you are the same. You have revealed yourself in Jesus Christ, the only begotten son. He comes to give us new life and new meaning to our living. Grant unto us the perception to understand what it is to be born anew. May we give ourselves to you in complete surrender. Let your spirit fill our lives and grant that in our finite minds we may love and adore you through your blessed son Jesus Christ, our Lord. Amen.

Something Dies, Something Lives

Scripture: *St. John 12:24*

> "Unless a grain of wheat falls into the
> earth and dies, it remains alone, but if it
> dies, it bears much fruit."

Meditation

    In the agro-industry as well as biological repro-
duction, there is a life and death process. The process of
germination of a seed requires air, warmth, and sun-
light. When this is lacking germination is impeded. The
seed must die before the plumule appears, after which it
begins to feed upon the nutrient of its host. Similarly,
Jesus refers to the cost of Discipleship. " He who
follows me and loves his life will not succeed. He who
loves his life, loses his life, and he who hates his life in
this world will keep it for eternal life." There must be a
dying process before one can find one's life in the
service of the master. This was the lesson Jesus intended for his disciples and all who want to follow him.

    He was about to lay down his life for the world
with the assurance that he would find it in the resurrection. The disciples and all believers must realize that
there is "death" in believing. The grain of wheat must
die before it can live and produce fruit.

    How are we doing in our Christian living? Have
we been dead to trespasses and sin? Are we living the
victorious life? How much fruit are we producing in our
witness for Christ? Do we see manifestations of this in
our own life, our interaction with family and friends,
co-workers, and people in our church and community?
Remember, there must be a crucifixion before a resurrection.

Prayer

Lord Jesus you have shown us the path of death to life in your death and resurrection. You have taught us, that in order to be your disciples we must, like the grain of wheat, die to self and rise to a new life. Enable us, by your grace to die to the Adamic nature in us and put on your nature. Equip us for service in the world by supplying the spiritual nutrients that will sustain us in this world of sin and strife. Lord Jesus, to whom we turn for guidance and hope, teach us to love you and to serve you and our fellow citizens. Grant us your peace and keep us, by your spirit, as we seek to witness to the world of your saving grace. Hear us and bless us this day as we pray in your name. Amen.

The Magnetism of the Cross

Scripture: *St. John 12:32-33*

> " 'And I when I am lifted up from the earth, I will draw all men to myself'. (He said this to show what death he was to die.)"

Meditation

The shadow of the cross is inevitable in the words of Jesus as recorded in this chapter of St. John. The anointing at Bethany is for "the day of my burial." The triumphal entry is made into Jerusalem. The crowds pressed to see Jesus. Jesus' reply to the Disciples is about the hour that has come for the son of man to glorified "unless a grain of wheat falls into the earth and dies, it remains alone; but if it dies, it bears much fruit. He who loves his life, loses it and he who hates his life in this world will keep it for eternal life. If any one serves me, he must follow me and where I am, there shall my servant be also; it any one serves me, the Father will honor him. Now is my soul troubled and what shall I say?" Father, save me from this hour? No, for this purpose I have come to this hour…and I, when I am lifted up from the earth will draw all men to my-self."

Jesus prepared himself for the cross. The cross was a punishment for criminals. It was introduced by the Phoenicians and taken over by the Romans. Criminals were tied to the cross, left hanging in the sun, sometimes for as long as three days. Ministering women were allowed to give them a sweet drink to deaden the pain and to arrest fatigue. Jesus intended to triumph over the horrible punishment and change the world. Out of suffering and death he would bring triumph and victory.

The cross of Jesus, like a magnet, has attracted and drawn men and women of all ethnic, cultural, educational, and regional levels for two thousand years and will continue to inspire and challenge the world until the end of time. It represents God's pure love, which initiates the pull on the sinful for their redemp-tion. God, in Christ is always drawing mankind to his love. Hence, the cross has universal appeal. Bunyan in Pilgrim's Progress describes the impact of the cross upon his life:

> "Thus far did I come laden with my sin,
> Nor could ought ease the grief that I was in,
> Till I came hither,
> Must here be the beginning of my bless?
> Must here, the burden fall from my back?
> Blest cross, blest sepulcher

> Blest rather be, the man that was put to
> shame for me."

Prayer

God our Father, the Father of our Lord Jesus
Christ, we praise you; we adore you for your love in the
redemption of the world by our Lord Jesus Christ.
Enable us to accept the cross and suffering of Christ
who became one of us in order that He could save us.
May we glory in the Cross of Christ and completely
surrender our wills to Him. Grant that in our witness
and daily living we will lift up the cross, which is the
means whereby others can be saved. Keep us near the
cross. Amen.

Cleansed by His Love

Scripture: *St. John 13: 1*

> "Truly I say to you, a servant is not
> greater than his master, nor is he who is
> sent greater than he who sent him."

Meditation

After Jesus had washed his Disciples' feet, he
taught them the relationship between the teacher and
the student. It was a lesson on humility. If he, being the
teacher and Lord, could wash their feet, even so should
they wash one another's feet. This was an example of
love. They should love one another.

Denominations of the Christian community
have practiced feet washing, especially on Maundy
Thursday. This is not regarded as an ordinance of the

church. However, Christians are exhorted to engage in this practice in love for one another. But love for one another goes beyond the practical act of feet washing. The love of Christ controls us .In our daily living this criterion should be the governing factor. The unselfish acts that we do everyday for our neighbors transcend feet washing. Charity rescues from the grave. Many individuals have been called to help their brothers and sisters who are less fortunate. Mother Theresa gave her life in the cause of helping the homeless, the diseased in India , and other areas in the world. The love of Christ calls us to such sacrifice for one another. If we are cleansed by his love, then we are to help one another. Are you cleansed by his love? How do you help the less fortunate in you community?

Prayer

God, our Father, we thank you for your cleansing and healing power in Jesus Christ our Lord. He has given us a practical demonstration of his love in the washing of the Disciples' feet. Help us as we show our love for each other in works of charity and mercy. Accept our praise and thanksgiving for all the faithful who have given service and their lives for the less fortunate and disadvantaged. Grant that the inspiration of their deeds may challenge us to serve our brothers and sisters in tangible and intangible ways. Create in us the spirit of love for the world in order that we may change it for the kingdom. Let brotherly love continue in our relationships. May we serve one another, through the love of Christ Jesus who gave himself for the world. Amen.

Let not your heart be troubled

Scripture: *St. John 14: 1-3, 25-27*

> "Let not your heart be troubled, believe
> in God, believe also in me...Peace I
> leave with you, my peace I give to you,
> not as the world gives do I give to you.
> Let not your heart be troubled, neither let
> it be afraid."

Meditation

Jesus in His farewell address to His Disciples
encouraged them to remove all fear from their minds
even though He would be physically absent from their
presence. He would not leave them comfortless or
desolate. They were to abide in His love and the Comforter, who is the Counselor, will instruct them in their
actions. He would come again and for that reason they
should have hope and be not fearful. When the Counselor, which is the Holy Spirit, is come, he will teach
them all things and bring all things to their remembrance. The crowning point is they will have peace.
This peace is not worldly peace, but the inner serenity
within each one, within their fellowship, and above all
with God.

Jesus is not absent from the world, though the
world anticipates his final return. He is omnipresent,
through the Holy Spirit, which came to the church on
the Day of Pentecost. But there is a futuristic appeal to
His message of comfort. He will come again for His
own. Are you His own? Do you expect His return? Do
you have peace within and are you praying for the
peace of the world? We must not be afraid. Christ is in
the world encouraging us in our daily pilgrimage. Let
us walk the way of faith, believing in Him for strength

and knowing that perfect love cast out all fear. This is the love of God through Christ Jesus our Lord.

Prayer

God, Creator, Redeemer, and Savior; In Jesus Christ you have given me peace. Accept my thanks and gratitude for sacrifice and promise of assurance of the Holy Spirit. You are one. Help me to accept this promise. Grant peace to each individual that calls on you, to the leaders of the world, and to all people throughout the world. Save us from war and pestilence. Grant us comfort in your word and love, and bless us this day through Jesus Christ. Amen.

For Their Sake I Consecrate Myself

Scripture: *St. John 17:19*

"For their sake I consecrate myself that they also may be consecrated in truth."

Meditation

Consecration is the work of the Holy Spirit. One does not consecrate ones' self; this is a work of grace in ones' life. But one must be in tune with the calling of the Holy Spirit in order to be consecrated for Holy Service.

Jesus in His high priestly prayer for his disciples prayed that they be united as one fellowship. He had given them the word. He would not pray that they be taken out of the world, but that they should be kept from the evil in the world. God should sanctify them in the truth. He would be leaving them, but also sending them into the world to perpetuate the truth. In order to continue his ministry, they must be sanctified.

It is for their sake that He is prepared to suffer. Such act of sacrifice requires his complete surrender of life. This is a hard commitment, but God will give the needed grace and strength.

Many individuals have witnessed consecration services or ordination of bishops, priests, elders, deacons, and baptisms within the Christian community. In some instances, prior to the act of consecration, the candidate for consecration withdraws from the world to a cloister where he meditates in seclusion in order to understand the solemnity of the ceremony that will set him apart for service to the world. It is for their sakes that one is consecrated. The outpouring and indwelling of the Holy Spirit separates the one that is consecrated for this life long service.

We may not be called to high office in the hierarchy of the church. Each one of us is called to life long commitment to Christ and ministry to the world. Whatever our calling, we must be consecrated by the Holy Spirit, if we are to serve in Truth. What is your calling? How do you serve the world?

Prayer

> Jesus calls us o'er the tumult,
> Of our lives' wild, restless sea:
> Day by day His sweet voice soundeth,
> Saying Christian, follow me.

Lord Jesus, we thank you for your consecration for us sinners. The suffering on the cross, death, and burial could not deter you. You gave your life for us and call us to follow you in love and service. Enable us by your spirit and grace to deny ourselves and take up the cross and follow you. May this be evident in our service to the sick and suffering, the down-trodden and dispossessed, the literate and illiterate, the employed and unemployed, the healthy and diseased and all others in their need. Sanctify us for their sake and for your service. We offer this prayer in your name, the suffering servant and Lord. Amen.

That They May All Be One

Scripture: *St. John 17: 20-21*

> "I do not pray for these only, but also for those who believe in me through their word. That they all be one, even as the Father art in me and I in Thee, that they also may be in us."

Meditation

St. John, Chapter 17 is regarded as the High Priestly prayer of Jesus. In this chapter he intercedes for the disciples as well as the future of the church. The central concern of Jesus is the unity or oneness of his followers.

The ecumenical movement began with this central theme – unity. But unity is not uniformity. Denominations of the Christian church have been separated by Dogma and creeds. In the interpretation of the scripture, many ideas and beliefs have caused divisiveness in the Church. The church of the Lord Jesus Christ is one, but many. When the "many" come together under one roof they establish a common faith. This accomplishment is by the Holy Spirit that binds us

together as one people around the world. Individuals of all rank and file, come together in one spirit to form the body of Christ. This becomes the fulfillment of Jesus' prayer that they all may become one.
When the church becomes one it can rightly minister to a divided world with the message of peace, love, and reconciliation. What are you doing to establish this oneness in Christ?

Prayer

O Jesus, the head of the church and Lord of all, we thank you for the gift of your spirit to the church. We thank you that your concern for its future has brought us to the unity of spirit that we enjoy. But Jesus, we have not lived our creed in many instances. We have fractured the faith by our unwillingness to fellowship with others of the faith. Save us, we beseech Thee, from discrimination and failure to work with one another. Heal the divisions of the church and create a fellowship of love throughout the universal church. Strengthen the weak, grant courage to the faithful and enable us all to seek your forgiveness, for the sins of disunity and grant us thy peace in the name of the Father, Son, and Holy Spirit. Amen.

Feed my Lambs, Tend my Sheep

Scripture: *St. John 21: 15-16*

"Jesus said to Simon Peter, 'Simon, Son of Jonah, do you love me more than these?' He said to him, 'Yes Lord, you know that I love you.' He said to him, 'Feed my lambs.' A second time he said to him, 'Simon, son of Jonah, do you love me?' He said to him, 'Yes Lord, you know that I love you.' He said to him, 'Tend my sheep.'"

Meditation

Most of us are familiar with the story about the relationships between Jesus and Peter. At their first meeting Jesus called him Petra – a rock – because he saw in him a strong character. It was Peter who wanted to build three Tabernacles on the Mount of Transfiguration after he witnessed the manifestation of Jesus' glory. It was Peter to whom Jesus would give the keys to the kingdom in order that he could 'bind or loose' on earth. Whatever he did on earth in this regard would follow in heaven. It was Peter who cut off the soldier's ear in the garden of Gethsemane. It was Peter who swore that he did not know Jesus while he was questioned in the judgment hall. It was Peter who accompanied the beloved disciple to the sepulcher on the resurrection morn. He was the impetuous one, yet, Jesus wanted him to feed His lambs, tend His sheep. He was not rejected by Jesus. The fisherman would not return to his fishing net. He was to prove his love for the souls of men and women; and from now on, feed the flock of God. Do you love me more than your present job? If you do, then come follow me, feed my lambs, tend my sheep.

Such a call proved true for Peter on the Day of Pentecost. At his defense of the cross and resurrection, three thousand souls were added to the church. Jesus may be calling you into his service. Listen to His voice and do His command. Feed my lambs, tend my sheep.

<u>Prayer</u>

Lord, you called Peter and others to do your
service and ministry. You have called individuals from
their vocations and professions to feed your lambs, tend
your sheep. Grant unto us the knowledge of your
presence and the willingness to respond to your call.
Enable us to be of service to the people we come in
contact with each day. If it is your will to send us on the
mission field as pastors and evangelists, administrators
and advocates, ministers in science and technology,
teachers and educators, doctors and nurses, parents and
guardians…whatever be our commitment, may we
serve you in spirit and in truth. Help us to care for the
lost sheep and to instill in them your love. We ask this
in the name of Jesus our Lord and Christ. Amen.

LENTEN MEDITATIONS

The Seven I Am Statements

I Am the Bread of Life

Scripture: *St. John 6: 32-35*

> "Jesus said to them, 'Truly, truly, I say to you. It was not Moses who gave you the bread from heaven. My father gave you the true bread from heaven. For the bread of God is that which comes down from heaven and gives life to the world...I am the bread of life: He who comes to me shall not hunger; and he who believes in me shall never thirst.'"

Meditation

Bread is an essential in the human diet. Jesus taught that man shall not live by bread alone. He fed the multitude with bread, an estimated number of four thousand and five thousand respectively. The day following the miracle, the disciples reported that all people were seeking Jesus and the Pharisees were asking for a sign referring to the manna, which their fathers had in the wilderness, which had come from heaven. Jesus' reply to them was "I am the Bread of Life." He is the true bread from heaven. Jesus is the inexhaustible source for the world. Blessed are those who hunger and thirst after righteousness for they shall be filled.

At the communion table bread represents His body; wine represents His blood.

"He who drinks shall never thirst, He

who feeds shall never hunger."
We sing the hymn.
Break Thou the bread of life, Dear Lord
to me,
As thou didst break the loaves, Beside
the sea
Beyond the sacred page, I seek Thee
Lord,
My spirit pants for Thee, O living word.

We need physical and spiritual bread for our
sustenance. We need not be Epicureans, but rather in
humility ask God: Give us this day our daily bread and
forgive us our trespasses (debts) as we forgive those
who trespass against us (our debtors).

<u>Prayer</u>

Jesus, you are the true bread from heaven. You
gave your life on the cross for me. Help me to appropriate your presence in the world as the living bread,
which sustains.

"Bread of the world in mercy broken,
Wine of the soul in mercy shed;
By whom, the words of life were spoken,
And in whose death, our sins are dead.
Look on the heart by sorrow broken,

Look on the tears by sorrow shed;

And be thy feast to us the token,
That by thy grace our souls are fed."

Lord Jesus, be Thou my daily bread, In the
name of the Father, Son, and Holy Spirit. Amen.

I Am the Light of the World

Scripture: *St. John 8: 12-18*

"Again, Jesus spoke to them saying, 'I am the light of the world, he who follows me will not walk in darkness, but will have the light of life…Even if I do bear witness to myself, my testimony is true, for I know whence I have come and whither I am going. You judge according to the flesh, I judge no one. Yet, even if I do judge, my judgment is true, for it is not I alone that judge, but I and he who sent me. In your law it is written that the testimony of two men is true. I bear witness to myself and the Father who sent me bears witness to me.'"

Meditation

Light is indispensable to living. It is a source of energy. It is a source of life to plants and animals. Light dispels darkness, reveals guilt, removes fear, and reveals impurity. The light of the sun, moon, and stars are wonders of creation. Electricity creates the means of livelihood and supports human development. Jesus is the source of energy and life to the church and the Christian. He is the pure and eternal light. He who follows Him will not walk in darkness, but will have the light of life.

The disciples are called to be the light of the world. Their light must shine in the world so that others may see their good works and glorify the father in heaven.

The great candle has been lit and from this,

other candles have carried the flame around the world.
You and I are like the Olympic runner that carries the
torch around the world bearing the good news that
Christ is the Light of the world and individuals should
no longer walk in darkness.

Although modern technology has introduced the
world to new techniques, yet there are areas of darkness
and ignorance remaining in our world. In order for this
darkness to be removed, we must exert our influence on
society. It will take some time for our prayers and
witness to become effective but we must not fail in our
commitment to Christ and the good news of salvation.
May God grant us the wisdom and skill to be lights in
this world.

Prayer

"Eternal light, Eternal light,
How pure the soul must be,
When placed within thy searching sight
It shrinks not, but with calm delight
Can live and look on Thee.

Guide me O God this day, that I may walk in the
light and be the channel of blessing to bring light at
home, with my family and friends, as well as my co-
workers and individuals in my community. Hear my
prayer in the name of Jesus Christ who is the Light of
the world. Amen.

I Am the Door

Scripture: *St. John 10: 7-9*

"Truly, truly, I say to you, I am the door

of the sheep. All who came before me are thieves and robbers; but the sheep did not heed them. I am the door; if anyone enters by me, he will be saved, and will go in and out and find pasture."

Meditation

Jesus uses the door as a figurative expression about our salvation. The door is linked with the role of the shepherd. He opens the door for the sheep. The door has many purposes and inferences

The door is entrance. It is to lock in and let out. It reveals a sense of ownership to the house. The one who turns the key is in possession of the house. A house without a door is a public thoroughfare. Door lends beauty to the home.

In life there are many doors; the door of opportunity, the door of frustration, the door of hope, the door of self-fulfillment, the closed door, the open door, and the door of salvation are examples.

Jesus Christ is the door of Salvation. The entrance to salvation is through Him. Those who enter will find pasture. This is the measure of grace that is afforded us in our daily pursuit. The artist portrays Jesus as knocking at the hearts' door. The doorknob is inside. You are to open the door and let Him enter.

Prayer

O Savior of the world, I open my heart to you this day. I know that you are with me. Take control of my life and be my guide and strength. Be my shepherd and lead me to pastures of righteousness. Enable me to

find joy in your service and fill me with your spirit this
day and always. Amen.

I Am the Good Shepherd

Scripture: *St. John 10: 11-15*

> "I am the good shepherd. The good
> shepherd lays down his life for the
> sheep. He who is a hireling and not a
> shepherd, whose own the sheep are not,
> sees the wolf coming and leaves the
> sheep and flees and the wolf snatches
> them and scatters them. He flees because
> he is a hireling and cares nothing for the
> sheep. I am the good shepherd. I know
> my own and my own know me. As the
> Father knows me and I know the Father
> and I lay down my life for the sheep."

Meditation

The role of the shepherd is to care for the sheep.
He is to find pasture for the sheep. The psalmist in
Psalm 23 wrote:

> The Lord is my shepherd, I lack nothing. He
> makes me lie down in green   pastures. He leads me
> beside still waters. He restores my soul. He leads me in
> paths of righteousness, for his names' sake. Even
> though I walk through the valley of the shadow of
> death, I will fear no evil, for thou art with me. Thy rod
> and thy staff, they comfort me. Thou preparest a table
> before me in the presence of my enemies, Thou
> anointest my head with oil, my cup overflows. Surely,
> goodness and mercy shall follow me all the days of my
> life, and I will dwell in the house of the Lord forever.

Jesus is the Good Shepherd. He gave his life for us in order that we may live. Throughout the centuries He searches out for us like a shepherd seeking the one lost sheep. Isaiah said, "All we like sheep, have gone astray. We have turned, everyone, to his own way. And the Lord has laid on Him the iniquity of us all." (Isaiah 53: 6)

We need to turn to the Good Shepherd and let Him lead us in pastures green.

Prayer

Eternal God, I thank you for sending Jesus into the world to offer his life as a ransom for my soul. He gave his life in order that I may live. Lead me beside the still waters; lead me in the paths of righteousness. Even though the valley of death comes my way, let me fear no evil. Sustain me with your goodness and mercy and give me the assurance that you are with me this day and always. You are my shepherd and I will follow you. Amen.

I Am the Way, the Truth, and the Life

Scripture: *St. John 14: 6-7*

"Jesus said to him, 'I am the Way, and the Truth, and the Life; no one comes to the Father, but my me. If you had known me, you would have known my Father also, henceforth, you know Him and have seen Him.'"

Meditation

In his farewell discourse with his disciples Jesus met with uncertainties about his functions and relationship with His Father. Thomas presented his doubts about His departure to prepare a place for His disciples. "Lord, we do not know where you are going, how can we know the way?" Jesus replied, "I am the Way and the Truth and the Life."

The Way is described as the Path or the manner of life. Christians were called the people of the Way. They are to enter by the narrow gate, for the gate is wide and the way is easy that leads to destruction. The gate is narrow and the way is hard that leads to life and those who find it are few.

The Truth is fact, what is real, what is right. It is opposite to falsehood or speaking lies. It is a virtue. Christ is the Truth. The word became flesh and dwelt among us full of grace and Truth and we beheld his glory; the glory of the only begotten Son from the Father.

The Life. This is animate as opposed to death. Jesus is described as the bread of life, the light of life, the resurrection and the life. Those who believe in Him shall never die. In John 10: 10 he said, "I am come that they might have life and have it abundantly." This is the life that we need as we embrace the Truth and walk in the Way. Let Christ be the Way that leads us to God.

Prayer

> "O Thou by whom we come to God
> The Life, the Truth, the Way,
> The path of prayer thyself has trod
> Lord, Teach us how to pray."

Father Almighty, Creator, Redeemer, and Friend, accept the prayers I offer for your enabling grace, which calls me, strengthens me, sustains me and will keep me on the path of service in your name. Be to all people the Way, the Truth, and the Life, and by your grace, keep us in your care through Jesus Christ our Savior and Lord. Amen.

I Am the Vine

Scripture: *St. John 15: 1-5*

> "I am the true vine and my Father is the vine dresser. Every branch of mine that bears no fruit, he takes away and every branch that does bear fruit he prunes, that it may bear more fruit...As the branch cannot bear fruit by itself unless it abides in the vine, neither can you, unless you abide in me. I am the vine, you are the branches. He who abides in me and I in him, he it is that bears much fruit, for apart from me you can do nothing."

Meditation

In his farewell discourse, Jesus took the agricultural approach. The grapevine is common in Palestine. Palestine is the home for grapes and vineyards. Jesus, as the teacher, moves from the known to the unknown. The vine is a trailing or climbing plant. In his teaching, Jesus made it clear that He is the vine, his Father is the vine dresser and the Christians are the branches. The three are inter-related.

The metaphor of the vine, vineyard, and vine dresser is one of caring, sharing, and producing. Pruning is for more productivity. The harvest of fruits (grapes) is anticipated. The interdependence and reciprocity of love is also illustrated. We are to abide in

Him as He abides in God. Abiding in Jesus offers
assurance for deeds to be performed, "Whatever you
ask shall be done." Jesus will even lay down His life for
you, for "greater love has no man than this, that a man
lay down his life for his friends." (John 15: 13)

<u>Prayer</u>

Heavenly Father, help me to see that interdependence between you, Jesus my Savior, and the Christian.
Enable me by your grace to be that Christian. I pray
that you will make me a productive witness of your
saving grace so that the world can be a better place.
Remove from me that which is unproductive and grant
that there will be a rich harvest as I do your work
through Jesus Christ my Lord. Amen.

I Am the Resurrection and the Life

<u>Scripture:</u> *St. John: 25-27*

"Jesus said to her, 'I am the resurrection
and the Life. He who believes in me,
though he die, yet shall he live. And
whoever lives and believes in me shall
never die. Do you believe this?' She said
to him, 'Yes, Lord, I believe that you are
the Christ, the Son of God, he who is
coming into the world."

<u>Meditation</u>

The raising of Lazarus is a miracle. Miracles are
the intervention of the supernatural in the finite world,
especially in human existence. Martha and Mary believed in immortality at the last day. Jesus assured them
that life after death is here and now. This is a cardinal

teaching of the fourth gospel and so Jesus declared that he was that new life. Even those who die the natural death will continue to live and those who are alone and believe will never die.

All religions teach life after death in one form or the other. There is a consciousness of spirit after death, whether in Elysian fields, Hades, Nirvana, or Paradise. The Christian religion teaches that eternal life begins here and now and is not terminated at death. Jesus is the resurrection and the life. Those who believe in him will enjoy continuous felicity with him in the hereafter.

St. Paul in writing to the Church at Corinth instructed them on the resurrection:
"Christ has been raised from the dead, the first fruits of those who have fallen asleep. For as by one man came death, by a man has come also the resurrection of the dead. For as in Adam all die, so also in Christ shall all be made alive." (1 Corinthians 15: 20-21)

Prayer
       God of the living, I come to you with the assurance that in the resurrection I will see Jesus my Savior and Lord. Accept my thanks and gratitude for your redemption in Jesus, the Christ. Help me by your grace to cast off the fears of death and hold onto the power of the risen Christ. Enable me to instruct others in the Truth of the resurrection and bring them to your saving grace. Help me to celebrate Easter in my own life, my home, and friends, through Jesus Christ. Amen.

THE SEVEN LAST WORDS

Father, Forgive Them for they know not what they do

Scripture: *St. Luke 23: 32-34*

> "Two others also who were criminals, were led away to be put to death with him. And when they came to the place, which is called the Skull, there they crucified him and the criminals, one on the right and one on the left. And Jesus said, 'Father, forgive, for they know not what they do.'"

Meditation

The Crucifixion of Jesus was a terrible crime. Crucifixion was introduced by the Phoenicians and taken over by the Romans. This was the harshest punishment that could be meted out to a criminal. Jesus was therefore treated like a criminal.

The charges of blasphemy and assertion of Divinity did not warrant crucifixion, but the scripture must be fulfilled. The prophet Isaiah had said, "He was wounded for our transgressions. He was bruised for our iniquities. Upon Him was the chastisement that made us whole and with His stripes we are healed."

Jesus taught His disciples to forgive and on the cross, He prayed for his enemies that God would forgive their ignorance. We too, need to forgive all who sin against us. We must remember that forgiveness is a divine injunction. If we forgive others, we will also be forgiven by God.

<u>Prayer</u>

Dear Lord and Father of mankind
Forgive our foolish ways
Reclothe us in our rightful mind
In purer lives Thy service find
In deeper reverence praise.

Almighty and loving Father, forgive me of all my sins. Here at the foot of the cross I lay my transgressions and pray for forgiveness. Hear my prayer for my brothers and sisters, relatives and friends; that you will blot out our transgressions and heal our souls through Jesus Christ who prayed for the world. Amen.

Today you will be with me in Paradise

<u>Scripture:</u> *St. Luke 23: 39-43*

"One of the criminals who were hanged railed at him saying, 'Are you not the Christ? Save yourself and us.' But the other rebuked him saying, "Do you not fear God, since you are under sentence of condemnation? And we indeed justly, for we are receiving the due reward of our deeds, but this man has done nothing wrong.' And he said to Jesus, 'Remember me when you come into your kingdom.' And Jesus said to him, 'I say to you, today you will be with me in Paradise.'"

<u>Meditation</u>

It must have been a shameful experience for Jesus to be on the cross. Added to the physical pain is

the emotional and psychological pain that came in the
ridicule from the criminal beside him. The power he
proclaimed, the miracles he had affected, the office he
declared he had, are now empty and dishonored. A
fellow criminal expects him to use his powers. Does
this sound like temptation? "If you are the Son of God,
throw yourself down." But the penitent asks to be
remembered in the kingdom. Jesus' reply is immedi-
ate, "Today you shall be with me in Paradise." So it is
for all who come to God through Jesus Christ in
penitence and humility. He will forgive our sins and
give us victory. We need to believe in Him and the
result will be forgiveness of sins and the reward of
eternal life.

Prayer

Great God, we thank you for Jesus, who was
punished for our sins and suffered a shameful death to
rescue us. We praise you for the trust we have in Him,
for mercy undeserved, and for love you pour out to all
people. Give us gratitude, O God, and a great desire to
serve you, by taking our cross, and following in the
way of Jesus Christ our Savior. Amen.

Woman, behold your son, Son behold your mother

Scripture: *St. John 19:25-27*

"Standing by the cross of Jesus, were his
mother and his mother's sister, Mary, the
wife of Cleopas, and Mary Magdalene.
When Jesus saw his mother and the
disciple whom he loved standing near,
he said to his mother, 'Woman, behold
your son.' Then he said to the disciple,
'Behold your mother.' And from that

hour the disciple took her to his home."

Meditation

Throughout the ages women have stood with their families, their children in trials and agony, in tragedy, and none have excelled Mary. In the agony on Good Friday, she stood at the foot of the cross and watched her son. The Roman Church has venerated Mary – as Holy Mary, Mother of God.

Before He breathed his last, Jesus took care of His mother. He made provision for John to take care of her. This was a Jewish custom for the eldest son to care for his mother, in death of the father. The absence of Joseph at the cross suggests that he had predeceased Mary. John is selected to carry out this task.

Jesus not only provides for Mary from the cross, but he provides for us by His grace. He cares for us in His redeeming love. He cares for all, irrespective of our status in life. He also asks us to care for one another in this life.

Prayer

Lord, we thank you for loving and caring mothers whose love and affection has changed the world. We thank you for Jesus, John, and Mary, and the work of grace in their lives and ours. Help us to care for our mothers and walk in the way of righteousness. Let your blessing be upon each child, mother, father, and family this day. In Christ name we pray. Amen.

My God, My God, Why Hast Thou Forsaken Me?

Scripture: *Matthew 27: 45-50*

> "Now from the sixth hour there was darkness over all the land until the ninth hour. And about the ninth hour, Jesus cried out with a loud voice, 'Eli, Eli, lama sabach-tha-ni, this is My God, My God, why hast thou forsaken me?'"

Meditation

The cry of dereliction from the cross echoes the words of the psalmist in Psalm 22: 1, 6-7. The psalmist had taken comfort in God's protection. His cry was:

> "My God, My God, why hast Thou forsaken me?
> Why are Thou so far from helping me
> from the words of my groaning?
> I am a worm, and no man
> Scorned by men, and despised by people
> All who see me mock at me
> They make mouths at me, they wag their heads."

Jesus was betrayed, denied, and forsaken by his disciples and God. The crucifixion had done its worst. Tired, hungry, thirsty, victim of fatigue and desertion by his friends, He cried out for divine help. We cannot identify with the cross of Jesus by dying for the world, but each one has a cross to bear as we go through life. Moments of despair, estrangement, disillusionment, frustration, and depression; at such times God appears to be far removed from us. Like Jesus, let us believe that He will deliver us.

Prayer

<u>O You Who Come</u>
Who are the hope of the world, Give us
Hope.
Give us hope that beyond the worst the
world can do
There is such a best that not even the
world can take it from us
Hope that none whom you have loved is
ever finally lost, not even to death.

<u>O You Who Died For Us</u>
In loneliness and pain, suffer to die in us
all
That keeps us from you and from each
other
And from becoming as good and as
brave
O Lamb of God, forgive us

<u>O You Who Rose Again</u>
You Holy Spirit of Christ
Arise and lie within us now
That we be your body that we may be
Your feet to walk into the world's pain
Your hands to heal, your heart to break.
If need must be for love of the world
O Risen Christ, make Christ in us All.
Amen.

(Anonymous)

I Thirst

Scripture: *St. John 19: 28-30*

> "After this, Jesus knowing that all was now finished said, (to fulfill the scriptures), 'I thirst.' A bowl full of vinegar stood there, so they put a sponge full of vinegar on hyssop and held it to his mouth. When Jesus had received the vinegar he said, 'It is finished.'"

Meditation

Thirst is a distressing sensation of dryness in the mouth and throat caused by want or need of fluids. It is the physical condition resulting from the want of liquid caused by dehydration or fatigue.

The humanity of Jesus revealed that he was hungry, he wept, experienced sorrow, often prayed, he was tired, thirsty, and died on the cross. The divinity of Jesus revealed in the incarnation statements about the Son of God, the giver of eternal life and the inexhaustible source to the world even the bread of life (John 6:35), the water of life (John 7:37-38).

The strange phenomenon is that the Son of God who gives living water is crying out for thirst on the cross. He needs to quench his thirst. But the thirst of Christ on the cross is more than physical. It is a spiritual thirst for the salvation of the world.

> I heard the voice of Jesus say
> Behold I freely give
> The living water thirsty one
> Stoop down and drink and live.
> I came to Jesus and I drank

Of that life giving stream
My thirst was quenched, my soul re-
vived,
And now I live in Him.

Prayer

Holy God, Father of our Lord Jesus
Christ
Your mercy is more than our minds can
measure
Your love outlasts our sin.
Forgive our guilt and fear and anger
We pass our neighbors in distress
And we are insensitive to the needy
We are quick to blame others, slow
Making up, and our resentment festers
Have mercy on us, God have mercy on
us, who blindly live our lives
For we do not know what we are doing
Destroy sin and pride, and renew us
By the love of Christ, who was crucified
for us. Amen.

It is Finished

Scripture: *St. John: 19:30*

"When Jesus had received the vinegar,
he said, 'It is finished and he bowed his
head and gave up the ghost.'"

Meditation

It is finished is not a cry of defeat or exhaustion,
despite the horrors of Via Dolorossa – the way of the
cross of suffering. It is a cry of accomplishment and

victory. It is the culmination of a human life, but more so it is the expression of satisfaction, that despite the odds, the persecution, the brutality on the way to the cross, and the murder, God's great plan for the redemption of the world is accomplished.

The words of James Montgomery remind us:

> "Calvary mournful mountain climb
> There adoring at His feet,
> Mark that miracle of time
> God's own sacrifice complete,
> It is finished hear him cry
> Learn of Jesus Christ to die

The drama of salvation from Eden to Calvary is climaxed in the sin bearer. All previous acts of God's redemptive love have reached their crescendo in Calvary. Jesus became the cosmic drama. Calvary is now center of the world, binding East and West, North and South, all ethnic groups, all nations, all people, you and me, in a harmony of love.

Prayer

Dear God We thank you for Christ Jesus our Lord and Savior who completed the work of Redemption in order that we may come to you. Grant that your grace will continue to sustain us in our deepest moments. Enable us to appropriate the sacrifice of Christ on the cross. May we be messengers of the finished and unfinished work of grace that is operative in the world. Bless all who work this day. Let your benediction be on all of your children. Amen.

Father Into Your Hands I Commit My Spirit

Scripture: *St. Luke 23: 46*

> "Then Jesus crying out with a loud voice said, 'Father, into your hands I commit my spirit.' And having said this he breathed his last."

Meditation

The story of our salvation falls into three segments; covenant, commitment, and commission.

The covenant is more than an agreement or contract. It is usually sealed with blood. In the Old Testament the life is in the blood. Jesus entered into a life giving, life saving experience with God and now that the work is finished, he deems it necessary to hand over everything to God.

This reveals the depth of His commitment. He carried through the covenant without flinching. He was commissioned to do a task. This is to bring salvation, to redeem humanity even with the shedding of blood. He suffered on the cross and now He is ready to hand over to God his life. He cried, into your hands I commit my spirit and then he breathed his last. We too are commissioned to a particular task for the world. Let us not surrender in the face of adversity but rather continue to the end of our lives' journey to work for the transformation of home and family, neighborhood and society, culture and the world.

Prayer

Eternal and everlasting God, accept our praise for your steadfastness and faithfulness to your creation

and to us. We thank you that Jesus our Savior endured
the cross and overcame death...that he was always in
unity with you and could finally hand over or commit
his spirit to your keeping. Help us to follow in His steps
and be strengthened in our work that we too may be
privileged to hand over our spirit (lives) into your
hands. May your Holy Spirit cleanse our hearts and
equip us for the future with you, through Jesus Christ
our Lord. Amen.

THE POWER OF THE RESURRECTION

Their Eyes Were Opened

Scripture: *St. Luke 24: 31*

> "Their eyes were opened and they
> recognized him and he vanished out of
> their sight."

Meditation

St. Luke describes how Mary Magdalene, Joanna, and Mary, the mother of Jesus and the other women went to the tomb on the third day with spices to complete their preparation for burial, which the Sabbath did not allow them to do. These women were told by two men that they need not seek the living among the dead.

On that same day two men were on their way to Emmaus recalling the story of the Crucifixion, and suddenly a third person appeared and joined the conversation. He upbraided them for their unbelief and showed them how the scripture had predicted the suffering of the Messiah. From Moses through the prophets, in all the scriptures it was predicted that he should suffer.

When they came to the village, he appeared to be going further but they constrained him saying, "Stay with us for it is toward evening and the day is far spent." So he went in to stay with them. When he was at table with them, he took bread and blessed and broke it, and gave it to them. And their eyes were opened and they recognized him, and he vanished out of their sight. They said to each other, "Did not our hearts burn within us while he talked to us on the road, while he opened to us the scriptures?" After this, they returned to Jerusalem and told the eleven of their experience, for he was known in the breaking of bread. This is a frightening experience. It is one of awesomeness. You are talking about the crucified, he appears and travels incognito, then discloses himself in the breaking of bread. Your heart begins to burn within you and then he disappears. Is this to confirm the details of the resurrection that he had given to the disciples? They all did not expect him to die, much less to accept the resurrection. To them, immortality was on the Last Day. He would rise again, not now.

Easter is the story of the Risen Christ who is ever present in the world and within the church and Christian community. The story of Easter is not Easter bonnet, Easter bunny, new apparel, Easter lilies, the beginning of spring, the twittering of birds, the change of season, the new life to plants. Easter is the time of rejoicing in the Risen Lord. Easter is the mystery and it is hope. It is the rising from the grave of Christ Jesus. He became the first fruits of them that slept, for as in Adam all die, even so shall all be made alive. He is risen is the song of the Christian community.

Prayer

> Jesus lives, thy terrors now
> Can O death no more appall us,
> Jesus lives, by this we know,
> Thou, O grave can'st not enthrall us
> Hallelujah.
> Jesus lives, for us He died,
> Thou alone to Jesus living,
> Pure in heart may we abide,
> Glory to our Savior giving
> Hallelujah

Omnipresent Savior, shine within our hearts this day and always. Amen.

The Ascension

Scripture: *Acts 1: 9-11*

> "And when he had said this, as they were looking on, he was lifted up, and a cloud took him out of their sight...will come in the same manner as you see him go into heaven."

Meditation

The ascension, like the Incarnation, is very difficult to understand. It is a mystery and we cannot unravel a mystery. We must apply faith over reason if we want to grasp an understanding of the working of God.

The Church has taught the ascension of Christ from its inception. During the New Testament period many believed that Christ's return was imminent. This belief would substantiate his ascension or departure. He had promised the Disciples that He would come again and receive them. They were to expect him at any time. This is a part of the Hope of Christianity. Christ will come again. What does ascension mean for us? Do we see Christ as the mediator who intercedes with God for us? Are we cynical that there was no ascension? If so, we would be called upon to account for his location in History.

The Church was empowered with the Holy Spirit ten days after the ascension. Should we bask in the advent of Pentecost, knowing that if Christ did not ascend, there would be no Holy Spirit, but that his ascension gave rise to the gift of the Holy Spirit to the Church. It s the belief of the Church that Christ will come again and for that reason it seeks to prepare individuals and the world to receive the good news of salvation and redemption.

<u>Prayer</u>

Jesus my Lord and Savior, accept my thanks and praise for your life on earth, your death, resurrection, and ascension. You have given yourself for the world and me. Grant O Lord unto me the faith to believe in the ascension and through your Holy Spirit come and set me free. May the Church await your return and may she ever proclaim your saving grace to the world. This I pray in your name. Amen.

Pentecost

<u>Scripture:</u> *Acts 2: 1-4*

> "When the day of Pentecost had come, they were all together in one place. And suddenly a sound came from heaven like the rush of a mighty wind…as the Spirit gave them utterance."

<u>Meditation</u>

Fifty days after the crucifixion and ten days after the ascension, the promise of the gift of the Holy Spirit was fulfilled. A group of one hundred and twenty followers of Christ waited in the upper room for the promise. "And suddenly a sound came from heaven like the rush of a mighty wind, and it filled all the house

where they were sitting. And there appeared unto them
tongues of fire, distributed and resting on each of them.
And they were all filled with the Holy Spirit and began
to speak in other tongues, as the Spirit gave them
utterance."

This manifestation created excitement in Jerusalem. The followers of Christ were charged with drunk-
enness. Peter became the champion and challenged his
hearers to accept Christ the Risen Savior and Lord, to
whom he attested this manifestation. The response to
his sermon was the in –gathering of three thousand
souls.

What does Pentecost mean to you? Do you
accept it as gibberish or the descent of the Holy Spirit
as Jesus had promised? The Church came into being at
Pentecost and since then has depended on the Holy
Spirit for its growth and development. What about
You? Have you experienced Pentecost? Are you born
again? Are you living the Spirit filled life? Does the
Holy Spirit govern your thoughts and actions?

Prayer

Spirit of the living God, fall afresh on
me
Spirit of the living God, fall afresh on
me
Break me, melt me, mold me, fill me
Spirit of the living God, fall afresh on
me. Amen.

Power to Witness

Scripture: *Acts 1: 8*

> "You will receive power when the Holy
> Spirit has come upon you; and you shall
> be my witnesses in Jerusalem and in all
> Judea and Samaria, and to the end of the
> earth."

Meditation

The struggle for power is a historical phenomenon. People power has been evidenced against absolut-
ism in France, autocratic rule in England, The French
revolution, the peasants revolt in Germany, the American revolution in the Colonies, the Haitian revolution,
the fight against apartheid in South Africa, and the
student power in Indonesia against the autocratic rule of
its President. "Power corrupts and absolute power
corrupts absolutely."

This is not the power that Jesus promised His
disciples. It was the power of the Holy Spirit, which
would unctionize them and send them forth as His
witnesses in all the world. Such an empowerment came
at Pentecost in the spring of A.D.29. One hundred and
twenty of His followers were waiting in the upper room
in Jerusalem for the promise of the Holy Spirit. Like a
mighty rushing wind the Holy Spirit descended on
them, filled the place where they were sitting, sat on
each person's head as cloven tongues of fire, and gave
them authority to speak in tongues. This is the power
that we need today in our assembly. It is not advocated
for speaking in tongues; rather it is to be empowered
with the gift of the Holy Spirit.

The gifts are many and varied, but when that

endowment is discovered it must be used for God's glory and the extension of His kingdom on earth. In this we witness to the fact of His saving grace in Jesus Christ, beginning with ourselves., drawing reference to the work and testimony of the Church in the world, and calling others to share in this missionary enterprises as they surrender their lives to Christ.

Prayer

God our Father, Creator and Sustainer. We thank you for the gift of the Holy Spirit. You have created the world and all that is therein. You have given us your Son Jesus Christ to be our Savior and Lord. You have sent us your Spirit to sustain us. Grant O God that we may be filled by your Spirit and be led by that Spirit into Christian service through out all the world. Enable us to visualize the world beginning with our environment and developing into the far corners of the earth. May we be channels of your grace to bring healing, comfort, love, and peace to our brothers and sisters at home, the workplace, the church, and the world. Sustain us by your Spirit through Jesus Christ our Lord. Amen.

The Cloud of Witnesses

Scripture: *Hebrews 12: 1-2*

"Therefore, since we are surrounded by so great a cloud of witnesses, let us lay aside every weight and sin which clings so closely, and let us run with persever-ance the race that is set before us, look-ing to Jesus, the pioneer and perfector of our faith, who for the joy that was set before him endured the cross, despising the shame, and is seated at the right hand of the throne of God."

Meditation

Life is like a race. We are all competitors in this race. Only those who see the end from the beginning will win the race. We are surrounded by the cloud of witnesses who ran in life's race before us. They seem to cheer us on as we progress in this relay. Even though extraterrestrial, yet they are watching our performance. This may seem strange to many people, but we do believe that those who ran before us and are now away from this physical world, do inherit the spiritual world and are a part of the mystic union with Christ. In so doing, they are with us in the Spirit.

In order for us to successful we must like the athlete, strip ourselves of the clinging folds. In the physical sense these are garments. Only the athlete's clothes will enable us victory. In the spiritual domain, the clinging folds of sin will trip us and cause us to loose the game. If we are to win the Christian race, we must fix our eyes on Jesus who despite the cross and its shame became the pioneer and perfector of our faith. He knew the joy of overcoming the horrors of the cross, death, and the glory of the resurrection. He is now at the right hand of God making intercession for all of us as we run the Christian race.

Let us therefore lay aside every weight that clings closely to us and run with perseverance the race that is set before us. Let us run as the Olympic athlete with our eyes on the prize. This prize is the crown of righteousness.

Prayer

Eternal God and Father of us all, accept our thanksgiving for sending your son into the world to be our Savior and Redeemer. You have called us to be your witnesses. Enable us to witness to the world of your love and kindness. May your saving grace be experienced by all and your kingdom be realized in the world. Accept our thanks for your faithful witnesses. Grant that their work will inspire us to be witnesses of your kingdom through Jesus Christ our Lord. Amen.

WHY WE BELIEVE

I Believe in God the Father Almighty, Maker of Heaven and Earth

Scripture: *Psalms 95: 1-7*

> "O Come, let us sing unto the Lord…
> O Come, let us worship and bow down
> Let us kneel before the Lord, our Maker
> For He is our God…sheep of His hand."

Meditation

All religions have God at the center. He is the indefinable source, the Absolute Truth, ultimate reality, infinite and ineffable.

Judeo-Christian religions use the terms omnipotent, omnipresent, omniscient, to describe the character of God. We come to believe in God by developing certain theological concepts. We talk about the cosmos in which God is creator/maker of the world. He is the all purposive, all sustaining, all goodness. He is Truth and Love.

The Apostles' Creed gives us a summary of the Christian beliefs. It affirms the Trinity, (Father, Son, Holy Spirit). Jesus taught His disciples to believe in God as Father. He loves, He listens, He cares, He heals, He is personal, and even agonizes with us in our pain and suffering. He is with us at the beginning and ending of life.

In times of stress and strain, in times of catastrophe and calamity, in times of success and prosperity, tin times of joy and in sickness and in health, God is there. "God is our refuge and strength, a very present help in trouble, therefore we will not fear."

St. Paul reminds us that He is not far from us, for in Him we live and have our being. This is the human and spiritual experience. You are asked to reflect on God's goodness in your life. You are asked to examine yourself in the light of what God has done for you in Jesus Christ, for God was in Christ reconciling the world unto Himself. This means that Christ's death on the cross is for us all. May we continue to believe in God, the Father Almighty, Maker of Heaven and Earth, giver of every good and perfect gift.

Prayer

God of the ages, you are from everlasting to everlasting the same God, You have given us the world, sustained us with your grace, given us your only Son to be our Lord and Savior, and fed us with your unfailing faithfulness. We thank you for your inestimable love in Jesus Christ. Help us to honor Him with our lives this day and always. Hear us as we pray for all classes and conditions of men; that they will respond to your call and obey you in service and love to each other, that a reign of peace may permeate our society, and friendship and brotherhood be established as we celebrate the love of one God, who is the maker of heaven and earth. This we ask in the name of Jesus Christ our Lord. Amen.

I Believe in Jesus Christ

Scripture: *St. John 1: 1-5, 14-16*

Meditation

The Apostle's creed attempts to summarize the life and work of Christ in these words; "Who was conceived by the Holy Ghost, born of the Virgin Mary, suffered under Pontius Pilate, was crucified dead and buried. He descended into hell, the third day He rose from the grave. He ascended into heaven and sits at the right hand of God, the Father Almighty, from whence He shall come to judge the quick and the dead."

The life of Jesus is filled with mystery. In the Incarnation, God inhabits the womb of a peasant woman. In his human development and growth, Jesus grew in wisdom. He was able to engage in analytical and philosophical discourse with the Rabbis when he was only twelve years old. His formal education was in the Rabbinical School. At thirty years he began His ministry and called the Disciples who left their occupations and followed Him.

This Divine-Human character has occupied the minds of people in the world more than any other. He is God and Man, philosopher, teacher, savior, redeemer, comforter, friend. He is the second person of the Trinity, wonder worker of miracles and lover of the human race. He is the archetype of the human race. He is perfect in all things.

As Redeemer, He goes the way of the cross and the new life that He offers to all who believe are indicative of His eternal claim to be the Son of God and the one who will come again for the faithful. Charles Wesley writes

> "Jesus, lover of my soul
> Let me to Thy bosom fly
> Other refuge have I none
> Hangs my helpless soul on Thee
> Leave, ah, leave me not alone,
> Still support and comfort me.
> All my trust on Thee is stayed

All my help from Thee I bring
Cover my defenseless head,
With the shadow of Thy wing."

Prayer

O Lord, Eternal and ever present, receive the prayers I make for your redeeming grace. O Jesus, Savior of the world, who gave your life on the cross that I may live, accept my thanksgiving for your undying love. O living Christ, who intercedes with the Father for me, plead my forgiveness this day so that I may be worthy to call on your name. Help me O Christ, to believe in your mercy and walk in fellowship with you this day and always. This I ask in your name. Amen.

I Believe in the Holy Spirit

Scripture: *St. John 16: 5-10*

Meditation

This is the third section of the Divine Triad, (Father, Son, and Holy Spirit). The world's living religions came into being by the Spirit. Hinduism speaks of the "Breath of God". Judaism describes the Spirit as the "Creative Spirit". Christianity recognizes the Holy Spirit as the Spirit of God. Jesus said, "God is Spirit and they that worship Him must worship in Spirit and Truth."

In the New Testament, the Holy Spirit is the Spirit of Christ. The Spirit invigorates and strengthens the church as well as the individual. It is the gift to the Church, otherwise known as the Comforter that comes alongside to comfort us on our earthly pilgrimage.

The Holy Spirit is a source of power. It is the animating force within corporate worship. It strengthens and sustains. It is to the Holy Spirit that we go for strength and by which we are sustained. Sometimes the work seems hard and difficult. We tend to give in or give up, but the Holy Spirit is there to sustain us. The Holy Spirit does not only strengthen and sustain, but commissions. At our baptism we sang:

> "O Jesus I have promised to serve Thee to the end,
> Be Thou forever near me, my master and my friend.
> I shall not fear the battle, if Thou art by my side,
> Nor wander from the pathway, if Thou wilt be my guide.

Jesus promised the Church the Holy Spirit; that promise is to you as well, "I will not leave you alone. I will send you the Comforter." He has done that. After His resurrection and before His ascension, he breathed on the disciples and said, "Receive the Holy Spirit." This is happening today.

Prayer

> Breathe on me breath of God,
> Fill me with life anew.
> That I may love what Thou dost love
> And do what Thou wouldst do.
> Breathe on me breath of God,
> So shall I never die.
> But live with Thee the perfect life
> Of thine eternity. Amen.

I Believe in The Holy Catholic Church

<u>Scripture:</u> *Ephesians 4: 4-6*

"There is one body and one Spirit, just as you were called into one hope that belongs to your call, one Lord, one faith, one baptism, one God and Father of us all, who is above all and through all, and in all."

<u>Meditation</u>

The Apostle's creed states that the Church is Catholic. This is the universal church that is above denominationalism. It is the "ecclesia" or those who have responded to the call of Christ to be His Disciples. The Church transcends time and space. It is invisible and visible, militant and triumphant. It is a fellowship of the faithful; otherwise know as the mystical body of Christ, incorporating the past, present, and future. It is also referred to as the company of the saints.

The Holy Catholic Church began at Pentecost when the Holy Spirit descended upon the group of one hundred and twenty in the Upper room who were awaiting the gift of the Holy Spirit, which was promised by Jesus to His disciples. Since Pentecost, the Church's ministry has extended throughout the world by those who are called to preach the good news.

The Church is an extension of Christ on earth. The Mission of the Church is to make Christ real to people. This is the gospel. This gospel comes to us through education and social concern, medicine, psychotherapy, agriculture, industry, thrift, justice, humanitarian services, rehabilitation and reconciliation, peace and brotherhood.

The call of the Church in contemporary time is to bring people into a saving/living relationship with God and His Son, Jesus Christ. We need Christ, we need the Church. We need to share our love with Christ and with people around us. If we believe in the Church, let us support the Church.

Prayer

Christ, you are the head of the Church; we are the members of your mystical body. Grant us light and truth to discern the true meaning of the Catholic Church. Through our ecumenical endeavors, grant that we may transcend national ethnic, geographical, regional, and social barriers and reach out into fellowship to praise you as one Lord, one God, and one Father of us all. Teach us to humble ourselves before you and seek ways in which we can strengthen our fellowship in the Church. Grant your Holy Spirit to each person who names your name and lead us, O King Eternal, to the perfect day, when we shall see you in your glory. Amen.

I Believe in Forgiveness of Sins

Scripture: *St. Matthew 5: 9-15*

Meditation

Forgive us our debts, as we forgive our debtors
And lead us not into temptation, but deliver us from evil
If you forgive men their trespasses
Your heavenly Father also will forgive you, but if you do not forgive

their trespasses, neither will your Father forgive your trespasses.

Most of us are familiar with the statement "To err is human, to forgive is divine." Jesus taught His disciples something of the nature of God. God is the one who forgives sins. In so doing, He sets us free. Our sins are remembered no more. In a similar manner, we are to forgive one another of the wrongs they do to us. It is not the number of times we forgive that counts; it is the nature of our forgiveness.

In the Apostle's creed we affirm the belief of the Catholic Church that Christ intercedes for us and in His name, God forgives us. The Christian community emphasizes this dogma in every age and every day.

Forgiveness breaks down the wall of hostility and reconciles us with those who are enemies. Jesus forgave those who were crucifying him and prayed for them, "Father, forgive them for they do not know what they are doing." A similar example of forgiveness is with the deacon Stephen. When he was stoned by his accusers for blasphemy, he prayed for them, "Father, lay not this sin to their charge."

Prayer

Dear God and Father of our Lord Jesus Christ, we come to you in penitence asking you to forgive us of all our sins. We need to forgive our brothers and sisters for the wrong they have done to us. Help us to forgive them and obtain your mercy and love. Bless all who come to you confessing their sins. Enable us by your grace to worship you and magnify your name. This we ask in the name of Jesus Christ, our Lord and Savior.
                                        Amen.

I Believe, Help My Unbelief

Scripture: *St. Mark 9: 23-24*

> "And Jesus said to him, 'If you can, all
> things are possible to him who believes.'
> Immediately, the father of the child cried
> out and said, 'I believe, help my unbe-
> lief.'"

Meditation

We are called to affirm our faith every time we
repeat the Apostles' Creed. But even when these
affirmations are made, there is still room for doubt. We
do believe God, but there are times when we ask the
question, why? Why does this have to happen to me?
Why is God testing my faith in this manner?

We believe and yet disbelieve. After the transfiguration of Christ, Jesus met the father of the epilep-
tic. "Teacher, I asked your disciples to cure him, but,
they did not, if your can do anything, have pity on us
and help us." Jesus' reply, "All things are possible to
him who believes." Immediately the father of the child
cried out, "I believe, help my unbelief."

> I believe for every drop of rain that falls,
> a flower grows
> I believe that somewhere in the darkest
> night, a candle glows,
> I believe that in the great somewhere a
> prayer is heard,
> Every time I hear a newborn baby cry, or
> touch a leaf or see the sky,
> Then I know, why I believe.

Prayer

O Lord our God, how excellent is your name in all the earth. We thank you for the company of the faithful who have believed in your promises and love. Help us who are the living to express our faith in your loving kindness through your healing, strengthening, enabling, and saving grace. Pardon our disbelief and mistrust. We have taken for granted your grace. Forgive us O Lord, and help us to rely upon you in all our daily pursuits. Help our unbelief. This we ask in your name and for your sake. Amen.

GOD'S PROVIDENTIAL CARE

Creation

<u>Scripture:</u> *Genesis 1: 1-5*

> "In the beginning God created the heavens and the earth. The earth was without form and void. And darkness was upon the face of the deep; and the Spirit of God was moving over the face of the waters.
>
> And God said, "Let there be light" and there was light. And God saw that the light was good and God separated the light from the darkness. God called the light, Day and the darkness he called Night. And there was evening and there was morning, one day."

<u>Meditation</u>

God created the world and all that is. The writer of Genesis describes the beginning of time. The ultimate source of Spirit created the world. He is Eternal, timeless, and yet compassionate and loving toward his creation. His divine providence sustains the universe and will sustain you today and always.

<u>Prayer</u>

God who is eternal, God who is everlasting the same, be my strength and sustainer this day. Guide my steps, order my ways. Supply my needs. Fill me with sense of wonder at your majesty, the beauty and order of the world you created. Help me to follow and serve you by renewing my faith and confidence in your divine plan for life through Jesus Christ. Amen.

Jehovah Jireh

Scripture: *Genesis 22: 14*

>"Abraham called the name of that place,
>"The Lord will provide." "Jehovah
>Jireh" as it is said to this day, "On the
>mount of the Lord it shall be provided."

Meditation

Sacrifice is an integral part of all religions.
Human sacrifice was practiced in the Ancient Near
East. Archeological artifacts have revealed that such a
practice was a part of the religion of Ancient Canaan.

The story about Abraham and Isaac at Mount
Moriah is intended to put an end to human sacrifice.
Abraham is called by God to sacrifice his only legiti-
mate son. He and Issac set out for Mount Moriah,
where God would test not only Abraham's faith, but
Isaac's courage as well. While climbing up the mountain with his father, Isaac said to him, "Behold the fire
and the wood, but where is the lamb for the burnt
offering?" Abraham's reply, "God will provide my
son." He was about to offer Isaac in an act of sacrifice,
but the voice said to him "Do not lay your hand on the
lad, or do anything to him."

Abraham lifted his eyes and behold behind him
was a ram caught in the thicket by the horns. Abraham
went and took the ram and offered it as a burnt offering.
God therefore provided an alternative. There is always
an alternative with God. The Great provider is always
furnishing us with His blessings. He provided for the
world the One Great Sacrifice of love.

God has provided many things for us for which we are grateful: life, parents, family, education, scholarships, fellowships, inheritance, legacies, gifts, law and freedom, democracy, employment, housing, spiritual vitality, friends, Christian fellowship, are some of His provisions for us. We need to pause and reflect on His goodness in our lives. He is able. His faithfulness is from everlasting to everlasting.

Prayer

God, you have been the Great Provider. You have given us the world and its resources. You have given us your only son to be our sacrifice. He offered His life for us. Help us to honor Him with our life of commitment. Supply our needs from your everlasting resource. Grant that we in turn may provide for those in need. May we continue to draw from your bounty.

> "Thy bountiful care, what tongue can recite
> It breathes in the air
> It shines in the light
> It streams to the hills
> It descends to the plain
> And sweetly distills in
> The dew and rain."

> "Frail children of dust, and feeble as frail
> In Thee do we trust, nor find Thee to fail
> Thy mercies how tender, how firm to the end
> Our maker, defender, redeemer, and friend."

> Amen.

The Earth Remains

Scripture: *Genesis 8: 22*

"While the earth remains, seed time and harvest, cold and heat, summer and winter, day and night shall not cease."

Meditation

After the flood, God established a covenant with Noah. The covenant of the rainbow was to remind Noah and his successors that life goes on. The earth will not be destroyed and productivity will not cease. Noah and his sons were to "be fruitful and multiply and fill the earth." This was a new beginning for the faithful. God said, "When I bring clouds over the earth and the bow is seen in the clouds, I will remember my covenant which is between me and you and every living creature of all flesh."

God made a covenant with Noah. In Jesus Christ, He has made a New Covenant with the world. Whoever believes on Him shall not perish, but have eternal life. The physical earth remains despite changes, but God's eternal Presence also remains. He sustains His creation. He's got the whole world in His hand. There is seed time and harvest, summer and winter, cold and heat, day and night. In the midst of these changes there is constancy. God is constant. He will see us through the changes of life. Ecclesiastes 3: 1 reminds us that, "For everything there is a season and a time for every matter under the sun" and in Ecclesiastes 3: 14, "Whatever God does endures forever, nothing can be added to it, nor taken from it."

We need not be fatalistic, but faithful to God's word and deed. As the earth remains, even to a greater extent is "God's presence and love." Let us seek the Lord while He may be found. Call upon Him while He is near and prove His faithfulness as we travel through life.

Prayer

God, Creator, Sustainer, and Redeemer, accept our praise and thanksgiving for giving us a world in which to live and prosper. We thank you for your faithfulness to your creation and above all to us in your redeeming love in Jesus Christ. Continue your blessing on good earth. Reclaim us for yourself and mold us for your service. May we be true to the New Covenant in Jesus Christ, and endeavor to serve you in the ministry we perform to our brothers and sisters in the world, through Jesus Christ our Lord. Amen.

Burning But Not Consumed

Scripture: *Exodus 3: 3*

> "And the angel of the Lord appeared to him in a flame of fire out of the midst of a bush, and he looked, and lo, the bush was burning, yet it was not consumed."

Meditation

The Old Testament contains various phenomena that relate to the presence of God. There are mountains, clouds, wind, smoke, fire, water, and theophanies (angels and spirits). God acts in and through them in Israel's support and deliverance. These were representations of God in Canaan, even before the time of Moses.

After his flight from Egypt, Moses became a shepherd to his father-in-law, Jethro, the priest of

Midian. He led his flock to the west side of the wilderness and came to Horeb, the mountain of God. An angel of the Lord appeared to him in a flame of fire out of the midst of a bush. His curiosity led him to investigate the bush that burned but was not consumed. Moses was told not to advance any further for the place on which he was standing is Holy ground.

This was an awesome experience for Moses, as it would be for us. He was in the presence of God. All religions teach that sense of awe when believers approach Deity. Islam has its sandals at the Mosque. Each individual on entering the Mosque must leave the sandal at its threshold.

We need to be aware of God's presence in our approach to worship. Whether in the sanctuary, the closet in our homes, the office desk, or the play field, God is everywhere. Let us stand in awe of Him...Let us take time to worship and adore Him for "the place on which you stand is Holy Ground."

Prayer

O Lord God, we thank you for your presence in the world. Your Holy Spirit energizes our hearts. Enable us to feel that burning in us that does not consume, but illuminates. You called Moses and commissioned him out of the bush. Do something similar for us this day for leadership in church or state. May we be a blessing to all this day, through Jesus Christ our Lord. Amen.

__The Ten Words__

Scripture: *Exodus 20: 1-17*

> "And God spoke all these words saying,
> 'I am the Lord your God…or anything
> that is your neighbor's.'"

Meditation

I am not going to comment on each verse or
commandment, but ask that you read them and see in
what way(s) you have kept these commandments.
However, I am joining the historian in examining these
commandments as Covenant between God and His
people of choice. The first five commandments are
designed to safeguard the most essential relations
between God and man. God alone is to be worshipped.
He is One. Idolatry of every kind is prohibited, viola-
tions of the day of rest are to be avoided (the Sabbath is
to be hallowed). Devotion to parents is enjoined.

The second five commandments secure relations
within the community. There can be no wholesome
covenant existence without the exclusion of killing,
adultery, theft, false witness, and covetousness.

These Ten Commandments form policy legisla-
tion. They are not law in the customary sense of the
term at all. There is a distinction for procedural legisla-
tion. As members of the covenant we are to endeavor to
keep the law, but Grace is stronger than the law. Moses
gave to his people the law to instruct them. God, in
Jesus Christ, has given us His grace to sustain us. We
should allow His grace to help us in keeping the law
and living lives that are worthy of our calling. Remember, we belong to a New Covenant, the Covenant of
Grace through our Lord Jesus Christ.

<u>Prayer</u>

Dear God, we have failed to keep your law. In so many ways we have sinned against you. Our transgression is ever before us. We ask that you forgive us of our transgressions. We know you can do this in the name of your Son, Jesus, the Christ.
O Jesus Christ, plead our cause and heal us this day. Let your grace sustain us and enable us to serve you today and always. Amen.

Able to Overcome

<u>Scripture:</u> *Numbers 13:30*

> "Caleb quieted the people before Moses and said, 'Let us go up at once and occupy it, for we are well able to overcome it.'"

<u>Meditation</u>

The earliest form of espionage recorded in the Bible and Israel's history is in this passage. In the conquest of Canaan, Moses resorted to the use of spies in order to test the strength of the Canaanites. The spies brought back the fruit of the land and told Moses that the land is fruitful and flowed with milk and honey, but the people are strong, the cities are fortified, and very large.

This was not discouraging to Caleb. He quieted the people before Moses and with confidence, inspired him to possess the land saying, 'We are well able to overcome.' Those who had gone as spies with Caleb and Joshua feared the Canaanites. They regarded the men as giants.

In our daily experience there are many challenges that come to us. We may not be called to military service and arbitration, but still we face problems that seem insurmountable and difficult to solve. Whatever is the problem, God, in Christ, can give us the solution. In Him, we are able to overcome. Jesus told his disciples, "In the world you shall have tribulation, but be of good courage, for I have overcome the world." (St. John 16: 33) We need to have faith and confidence in God.

Prayer

Eternal God and Father of mankind, we thank you for your guidance in the world. You have guided nations, kingdoms, and people in history. Your love is ever new. Guide us in our daily endeavors. We bring to you our problems of family, friends, and neighbors with the understanding that you will help them to overcome and have peace with God. Strengthen our faith and grant us courage for this day. We pray in the name of your Son, Jesus our Lord and Savior. Amen.

God Is First

Scripture: *Deuteronomy 6: 4-9*

> "Hear O Israel, The Lord our God is one Lord, and you shall love the Lord your God with all your heart and with all your soul and with all your might…your gates."

Meditation

Deuteronomy is a part of the Pentateuch. The first five books of the Old Testament form the Pentateuch. It is generally accepted that Moses is the

author of these books. There is not only a similarity in
Chapter 5 of Deuteronomy with Exodus, Chapter20, but
a repetition of the commandment and precepts that
should govern the life of Israel. But the Deuteronomist
goes further than written injunctions concerning loyalty
and love to Deity; he takes the practical approach to
worship, loyalty, and devotion to one God. If Monotheism is to survive, then the present generation and
generations yet unborn must practice the Shema...
"Hear O Israel, the Lord our God is one Lord, and you
shall love the Lord your God with all your heart and
with all your soul and with all your might. This means
you shall love God with all your being which is inclu-
sive of your attributes and endowments.

This passage has become the basis for Rabbinical teaching and the establishment of Religious Education in Jewish history. Jesus in his dialogue with the
scribe who inquired of him which commandment is the
first, reiterated what was familiar to him and said,
"There is a second commandment of equal value and
significance, you shall love your neighbor as yourself."
(St. Mark 12: 31)

The Reformer Martin Luther also emphasized
the relationship to God and the relationship to our
neighbors. The perpendicular and the horizontal relationship give us a right angle. This is symbolic of our
love to God and love to our neighbor. Love to God is
first, but it beckons us to love our neighbors. This love
is not written on phylacteries or inscriptions or amulets.
It is written in the heart. This kind of love is needed in
our world today. We need to practice more love for our
neighbors in the community, work place, and the world.
We do this because we first love God.

Prayer

Our God, you are the source of our love. In love, you created us, in love, you have redeemed us, and in love, you sustain us. Grant us the knowledge of your presence and the experience of your spirit that we may truly "love and serve you." Accept our thanks for your love in Jesus Christ our Savior, who so loved us that He gave his life on the cross to save us. Teach us to love you day by day and walk in the steps of Christ our Lord. Enable us to love our neighbors. Teach us to understand the ways in which we can love them as ourselves. In unselfishness may we be a blessing to them at work, in the neighborhood, and the community. Bless all our neighbors in Jesus Christ. Amen.

We Will Serve the Lord

Scripture: *Joshua 24: 15*

> "And if you be unwilling to serve the Lord, choose this day whom you will serve...but as for me and my house, we will serve the Lord."

Meditation

Judaism and Christianity are exclusive religions. Both have the underlying principle of Monotheism. Yahweh (Jehovah) is one God and there is no other. In the time of Joshua, polytheism was common belief in Canaan. Joshua realized that this was detrimental to the faith and a threat to Monotheism. In his farewell address to his people he warned them against the evils of Baalism and encouraged them to put their trust in Jehovah.

But if they failed to follow his admonition, then he would continue his trust in the one true God. He was responsible for his household and they would continue to put their trust in God. The head of each household had a responsibility to God for the religion of his family. This is lacking in our homes today. We need to rekindle in our homes the faith in God. The family altar and the family at worship ought to be an integral part of the home. Each member of the family needs to share in the corporate fellowship of the church. The family that prays together stays together. This maxim should guide our actions in the family as well as at the work place. We all need the Lord and need to serve Him wherever we are.

Prayer

O Lord, we bring to you our families. We ask that you will bless each family in whatever locale they may be established. Remove the barriers that separate and alienate the family members from each other. Grant direction and guidance to the head of the family in order that they may instill faith in their offspring. Bless the mothers, fathers, and children in our family. Lord, we pray for the wider family in the world. May we come to realize that we are of a common lineage and in our understanding create a fellowship throughout the world. Lord, you have called us as a church to the family of God. Rid us of prejudices, hatred, and bitterness and create in us the spirit of love for one another, in order that we may serve you in spirit and in truth. In your name we pray. Amen.

The Three Hundred

<u>Scripture:</u> *Judges 7: 6-7*

> "The number of those that lapped,
> putting their hands to their mouths was
> three hundred men, but all the rest of the
> people knelt down to drink water."

<u>Meditation</u>

During the period of confederacy in Israel, God
chose judges or charismatic leaders to lead the people.
Gideon was chosen after various tests. The test of
sacrifice in which the offering was consumed by fire,
the test of the fleece in which on one hand it was wet
and dry all around and on the other it was reversed.
Then came the summons for battle in which 33,000
responded. This was reduced to 10,000 and finally to
300. By the strategy of allowing men to drink from the
spring, Gideon eliminated most of the men. Only those
who lapped putting their hands to their mouths were
chosenThese, Gideon took to fight the Midianites.
Trumpet along with the Password, <u>the sword of the
Lord and of Gideon.</u> At the dead of night, while everyone in the camp of the Midianites was sleeping, Gideon
signaled his men to remove the torches from the jars,
smash the jars, wave the torches and shout, "The sword
of the Lord and of Gideon." The Midianites were
awakened to grave consternation and turned on themselves.

We can learn many lessons from this strategy.
The battle is not for the fearful and anxious, but for the
courageous and loyal. The password is the key to
success.

These are important in our daily living. We

struggle against principalities and powers against our inner feelings of anxiety, fear and cowardice, and think we will not achieve. We need to follow our Leader, Jesus Christ, and realize that faith is the victory that overcomes the world. Our success does not depend on numbers. The faithful will succeed.

Prayer

Eternal God and loving Father, we thank you that it is not by might or power, but by your spirit that we can attain success. In our weakness, make us strong. Take the faithful in our world and enable them to be courageous against the evils that confront us. Give us the password in Christ Jesus who is the Way, the Truth, and the Life. May we be true to Him in our daily living and witness. Strengthen the faith of all who call upon you, and grant us victory in our daily pursuits, through Jesus Christ our Lord. Amen.

Stand Tall

Scripture: *I Samuel 10: 22-23*

"Behold he has hidden himself among the baggage. Then they ran and fetched him from there; and when he stood among the people he was taller than any of the people from his shoulders upward."

Meditation

Saul was the son of Kish, of the tribe of Benjamin. He was a handsome young man. There was not a man among the people of Israel more handsome than he. From his shoulders upward he was taller than any of the people. Taken literally it presents the pre-requisite for an oriental monarch.

Even though he was anointed secretly by Samuel, yet he avoided the intentions of the crowd. He hid under the baggage. But when he was taken out he stood shoulder high above the people. Samuel said to the people, "Do you see whom the Lord has chosen?" All the people shouted <u>Long Live the King.</u>

History has shown that Saul was more of a charismatic leader than a king. He suffered from melancholia and had a tragic death. The spirit of God left him. He committed suicide in the battle against the Philistines.

What kind of leadership do we look for in our leaders today? Leaders are born, leaders are trained, and leaders are made. Which are you? Are you able to stand tall amidst the surging tide or the howling of the wind or the turbulence of the tide? Leadership is not physical attractiveness or sportsmanship. Leadership is character. Leadership is spiritual. This is where leadership stands tall. This is dynamic, creative, forceful, charming, astute, flamboyant, erudite, and above all leadership that possesses the love of Christ. So much of this is needed in our society whether we are administrator, educator, civil servant, Mayor, Governor, President, Pastor, or servant.

<u>Prayer</u>

Dear God and Father, you have created us for a purpose. We cannot all be leaders in church and state, but we can lead in other spheres. Help us to be faithful to our trust and lead in whatever area we are called to lead and serve. Let the Holy Spirit be our teacher and guide in order that we may lead your people in truth, honesty, and uprightness. Pour out your spirit upon all who hold high office, president, governor, mayor, members of Congress, parliament, the judiciary, education, government, and the civic community in order that we may all create a harmonious environment which will benefit individuals and enhance the true spirit of service and hasten the building of your kingdom on earth…a kingdom of righteousness and peace through Jesus Christ our Lord. Amen.

An Understanding Mind to Govern

Scripture: *1 Kings 3: 9*

> "Give your servant therefore an understanding mind to govern your people, that I may discern between good and evil, for who is able to govern this your great people."

Meditation

Solomon became King in succession to his father David. In as much as he loved the Lord, he sacrificed and burnt incense at the High Place in the land. It is obvious that religion was not yet centralized in Jerusalem. It was the temple that centralized religion in Israel and this was not yet built.

Early in his reign, Solomon set out to emulate his father. He confessed that he did not know how to govern the nation and wanted an understanding mind in order to govern the chosen people. God appeared to him in a dream with the request, "Ask what I shall give you". Dreams do have significance in our religious and cultural experience. Sigmund Freud places great emphasis on dreams. Most of us have had such an experience. After recalling God's great and steadfast love to

David, Solomon chose the wise and understanding heart above riches and long life. This is borne out in the wisdom literature that acclaims Solomon as the wisest at the time.

What does the understanding mind have to offer us? All of us who are in positions of leadership need a wise and understanding mind to govern or lead. This may be in the home or family circle, in the school as teachers, at the work place as employer or employee, in the legal and medical professions as practitioners, in the Church as pastors and administrators, in the government as counselors, representatives at state and national level, and as Vice-President and President at national level. From the least to the greatest we need an understanding mind to govern.

Prayer

God, you are sovereign ruler of the created order. You brought order, life, and meaning out of chaos. You have redeemed us from sinfulness and given us liberty and creativity. Grant that we may use our God-given abilities and endowments to lead your people in Church and state. We confess that we do not know how to govern. Give us wisdom, give us the courage to do the duties to which we are assigned, whether at home, work place, cloister, seat of government, or at the bench. Help us to wait on you for guidance and strength in order that we may govern (rule) in love with justice and righteousness, through Jesus Christ, our Lord. Amen.

What Are You Doing Here, Elijah?

Scripture: *I Kings 19: 9*

"And there he came to a cave, and

lodged there; and behold, the word of the
Lord came to him, and said to him,
'What are you doing here, Elijah?'"

Meditation

Elijah was the champion of religion in Israel
during the reign of Ahab and Jezebel. The struggle for
Yahweh's supremacy over the Baals of the land resulted in the controversy at Mount Carmel. Elijah's
God answered by fire and consumed the sacrifice that
the prophet offered.

He seized the opportunity to eradicate idolatry
in Israel by slaughtering the four hundred and fifty
prophets of Baal and the four hundred prophets of
Asherah. This caused Jezebel to become furious and
threatened the prophets' life. Elijah escaped to the caves
of Mount Horeb where he was sustained by God. But
he became despondent. He felt that he was the only one
in the land that remained faithful to god. "I even I only
am left and they seek my life to take it away."

After asking him, " What are you doing here,
Elijah?" God, in order to convince him that he was not
alone spoke to him through the phenomena of nature;
the wind, the earthquake, and the fire. Elijah did not see
the Lord in these. It was in the still small voice that
Elijah heard God's voice of reassurance. There were
seven thousand in Israel who did to bow their knees to
Baal. Elijah's despondency was changed to commission. His task was not finished. He was to anoint Hazael
as King over Syria and Jehu as King over Israel. Elisha
was anointed as his successor.

What beautiful lesson is portrayed in this passage? What are you doing here Elijah? So many times,
like Elijah, we struggle for religious piety and

ceremonials in a world that is hostile to God and Christ.
So many times, we think our witness is thwarted and
even our lives threatened .We become despondent and
resort to our "cave" .In such situations, God comes,
calls us, commissions us for the task of changing our
world with the reassurance that there are faithful ones
endeavoring to keep the faith, though they are unseen
and that our work is not complete. We are not alone.
Others are with us in the struggle for Christian virtue
and values.

Prayer

In silent mediation let us ponder the words of
the hymn by John Whittier:

> Dear Lord and Father of mankind
> Forgive our foolish ways;
> Reclothe us in our rightful mind
> In purer lives thy servant find
> In deeper reverence praise...
> Breathe through the heats of our desire
> Thy coolness and thy balm;
> Let sense be dumb, let flesh retire,
> Speak through the earthquake, wind, and
> fire
> O still small voice of Calm

Our Father and our God, remove from us despondency and frustration in our service to you and our
people. Strengthen our faith in you. Enable us to know
that your Spirit is with us in our endeavors and commission us for service in your name. Speak to us O still
small voice of calm, through Jesus Christ our Lord.
Amen.

Restoring God's House

Scripture: *2 Kings 22: 13*

> "Go, inquire of the Lord for me, and for
> the people, and for all Judah concerning
> the words of this book that has been
> found...to all that is written concerning
> us."

Meditation

Josiah began to reign when he was only eight
years of age. He is known for his restoration of
Yahwehism in Judah. Prior to his reign, the kingdom
was besieged by Baalism and cultus of various kinds.

In his reform the Deuteronomic code was found
in the house of the Lord. This was the book of the
covenant, which was not kept from the time of the
Judges. Josiah carried out a thorough reform. He destroyed the cultus and the altar at Bethel, which was
erected by Jeroboam who made Israel to sin. The
people were called upon to observe the Passover.
Religion was restored to Jerusalem.

Josiah is recorded as the Reformer who brought
Israel back to the covenant days with Jehovah. Is this a
strange phenomenon for us these days? Do we have
kings or rulers leading the nation back to God or the
covenant with God? The Christian religion is not a
political religion. It is free from political alliance
especially in countries where it is not a state religion.
Be that as it may, we all need to return to God. There
are so many "idols" in our culture, religious practices,
and our personal lives. We need to rid ourselves of

these idols and worship God in Jesus Christ. He has made God known to us.

Prayer

Eternal God and Father, you are the center of our worship and devotion. You have been revealed to us through your son, Jesus Christ. Help us to worship you in spirit and in truth. Give us due sense of your mercies in order that we may truly worship and serve you. You have made us a covenant people through the redeeming sacrifice of your son, Jesus Christ. Grant that we may turn from sin and any form of unrighteousness and worship you this day and always, through Jesus Christ our Lord. Amen.

The People Had a Mind to Work

Scripture: *Nehemiah 4: 6*

> "So we built the wall, and all the wall was joined together to half its height. For the people had a mind to work."

Meditation

Nehemiah is specifically identified by the chronicler as a high official in the court of Artaxerxes the King. The King granted his request to go to Jerusalem without asking a single question. There was a special affection for the homeland on the part of the Jews born in exile, even though they had never seen the land of their forefathers.

Nehemiah's heroic struggle to build Jerusalem's walls is one of the splendid narratives of biblical literature. He was faced with opposition from Sanballot and

Tobiah, but he persisted, believing that "our God will fight for us." (Nehemiah 4: 20) "We labored at the work and half of them held the spears from the break of dawn till the stars came out." (Nehemiah 4: 21)

After fifty-two days, the wall was completed. The people knew their work was accomplished by the help of God. With the assistance of Ezra, the walls were dedicated and reforms re-enacted to restore covenant worship in the land.

The important aspect of this reform is the peoples' attitude. They had a mind to work. They saw the need for restoration and they gave themselves to its accomplishment. They worked against the odds, following the instructions of Nehemiah. Do we have walls or structures to repair or rebuild? Are these physical and material or are these social, moral, cultural, economical, ethnic, or racial? Are these spiritual whether personal or corporate? What are the walls that separate us from each other and from God? We need to find out.

Prayer

Lord of all being, we thank you that there is no wall of separation between you and those who trust and serve you. But there are crumbling walls, dividing walls, and institutional structures that separate us as a people. There are walls erected by petty jealousies in our family and our relationships in our community and work. Remove these walls and unite us in the bond of love. Grant unto us the spirit of co-operation, responsibility, and service in order that we may build a community without walls. Strengthen our hands for this great work in Jesus' name. Amen.

I Know That My Redeemer Lives

Scripture: *Job 19: 25-26*

> "For I know that my redeemer lives, and
> at last he will stand upon the earth, and
> after my skin has been destroyed, then
> from my flesh I shall see God."

Meditation

Job is regarded as the greatest poetic work
produced by the Israelite community. As part of the
wisdom literature it seeks the answer to immortality.
The attacks on man's finitude may prevail but that is
not the end. After my skin has been destroyed, then
from my flesh I shall see God.

The Author takes as a framework of his poem a
quite ancient and no doubt popular narrative of a pious
man named Job whom Yahweh (Jehovah) tested and
afflicted to see if his faith would endure adversity. The
form of the poem is clearly that of a set of dialogues
between Job, his three friends, and his wife. In the end,
Job is victorious. He cries with exultation. I know that
my Redeemer lives and He will meet Him as He is on
the last day. He trusts the living God, the God of love
and righteousness, who alone can vindicate the cause of
man.

The story of Job's life may not be the story of
our lives. But do we have our problems? Certainly we
do. Are there times in our everyday experience when
the ground beneath our feet seems to be crumbling?
Yes, there are times. What about our failures, discour-
agements, loss of family member, house, land, property,
or health? We all seem to share in such experiences and

more. Have we reached the point to curse God and die? Then where do we go from here? The true answer to Christian faith is in the words of Job, "I know that my Redeemer lives and at last He will stand upon the earth. And after my skin has been destroyed, then from my flesh I shall see God."

<u>Prayer</u>

Our God, the Rock of Ages, we thank you for your faithfulness to your world. You have not left us to our finitude, to rot and decay, but in your love you have given us new life in Jesus Christ, our Redeemer. Accept our thanks for the gift of faith and eternal life. Strengthen our faith in these days of stress and strain, pain and suffering, and grant us the courage to continue our quest of eternal life with you. May we trust you and not curse you. May we give ourselves to your service and follow you in whatever we do. Take us by your hand and lead us on to life everlasting. Christ our Redeemer be in our understanding, in our going out and in our coming in form this day and forever. Amen.

Trust In The Lord

<u>Scripture:</u> *Proverbs 3: 5-6*

"Trust in the Lord with all your heart, and do not rely on your own insight. In all your ways acknowledge him, and he will make straight your paths."

<u>Meditation</u>

The admonition of the writer of Proverbs is applicable to everyone even though he selected the son as his addressee. He exhorts the son even as a father does with his son. The son is to seek wisdom and forget not the teachings of the father.

In the Shemah, the Hebrew son is to remember that the Lord our God is one. He is to put around his neck, arms, ankles, the words. He is to write them upon the tablet of his heart. And so in the proverbs he is to engrave wisdom. This wisdom is from God. In all his ways he is to acknowledge God. He is not to lean on his own insight. god will make his paths straight.

All knowledge and wisdom come from God. In our academic preparation, God is the source from which we understand. He gives insight or enlightenment and we recognize his hand in that revelation that gives us advancement. We become successful in examination, business profession, and vocation. It behooves us to trust in the Lord with all our hearts, our emotions, or psychic response. When we allow God to be the center of trust, the result is, we find favor and good repute in the sight of God and man. This is important in our everyday pursuits. To those entering school, college, or university, this is a priority, if we are to be successful. And to those in the other areas of life, this is also the most important aspect to our achievement.

<u>Prayer</u>

Lord, in a world that is competitive, we fail to trust you. We have compared ourselves with others and regard their success as unattainable. Grant to us the knowledge of your presence in all that we do in order that we may account for our success by your mercy and grace. Help us to gain insight into your plan for our lives. May we acknowledge you in whatever we do. Grant us success in school, college, university, and the work place. We ask that we do not forget your guid-

ance, help, and comfort in our pursuits. Grant that we
may find you and worthily magnify your name through
Jesus Christ our Lord. Amen.

Prove Me Now

Scripture: *Malachi 3: 10*

> "Bring the full tithes into the storehouse;
> and put me to the test says the Lord of
> Hosts, if I will not open the windows of
> heaven for you and pour down for you
> an overflowing blessing."

Meditation

The book of Malachi deals with the perversion
of the life of Judah by unworthy offerings, social evils
and by other acts of infidelity to the covenant. The
people weary Yahweh (God) with their misconduct,
their offerings of worthless gifts, and their robbery of
God himself. (Malachi 3: 6-12)

Like the teacher, the prophet raised the question,
will man rob God, and he answers the question, you are
robbing me. He goes on, but you say, how are we
robbing God, then he answers the question, in your
tithes and offerings. Finally, he exhorts his hearers to
bring the full tithes into the storehouse that there may
be food in my house and thereby put me to the test, says
the Lord of Hosts, if I will not open the windows of
heaven for you and pour down for you an overflowing
blessing.

Malachi is saying – prove me now. Put me to
the test and see what is your reward for giving. Be
sincere in your worship and in your giving. Give God a

tithe of your earnings and the windows of heaven will be opened to and for you. This is the crux of our giving. The tithe is one tenth of one's salary or earning.

Christian stewardship requires the tenth if the work of the church is to be accomplished. Everyone who tithes knows of the blessing of heaven. Both the giver and the receiver are richly blessed. Our giving is in grateful acknowledgement to God for his redeeming love in Jesus Christ, and that are gifts may be used in the extension of His kingdom to all mankind.

What about your giving to God? Are you robbing God? Do you need His blessing in your life? Then, give to Him your tithe and offering, your time and your talent. The blessings will be personal and corporate.

Prayer

Father, we thank you for all the blessings you have given us... for life, home and family, profession and vocation, for Church and community, for the nation and the world. We are conscious of your faithfulness. "Morning by morning, new mercies I see. All I have needed thy hand hath provided. Great is thy faithfulness, Lord unto me."
We give to you our tithes and offerings in material wealth, our time and talent in grateful acknowledgement of your love. Help us to sincere in our giving. Save us from robbing God. Accept our thanks for the many ways in which we have been blessed. Enable us to continue our gifts to your service, through Jesus Christ our Lord. Amen.

COMFORT THROUGH THE PSALMS

The Way of the Righteous

Scripture: *Psalms 1: 1-3, 6*

> "Blessed the man who walks not
> in the counsel of the wicked, nor
> stands in the way of sinners…for
> the Lord knows the way of the
> righteous"

Meditation

Righteousness is a strong Judaic-Christian
expression. It has great significance. It is synonymous
with Justice and Truth. To do what is right is to do what
is just, and this will result in an acquittal before the
court. The decision reached either by the individual
group, jury, or judge conveys "rightness" to the recipi-
ent. Justice not only appears to have been done, but is
done.

One comes to know righteousness from God's
acts. The nature of God is one of righteousness. Consequently, His acts are right. From this, we learn to walk
in communion with God. The person who delights in
the Lord and meditates on His law day and night is
likened to a tree that is planted by streams of water, that
yields its fruits in its season, and its leaf does not
wither.

The metaphor of the productive tree is applied
to the righteous. In all that he does he prospers. One
may question this is the light of the situation facing
many of us today. It appears as if the righteous have
more setbacks or disappointments than the wicked, but
above all the righteous can appropriate God's blessings

in his life. The righteous will stand in the day of judgment.

In a world of sin and strife this offers comfort and consolation to the righteous. We shall not perish, but attain our freedom in God. Let us therefore seek the way of the righteous for the Lord knows the conditions of that way.

Prayer

God of justice and righteousness, accept our praise for your faithfulness to your people. In Jesus Christ you have revealed your nature to us. We thank you that in him you acquitted us of our sinfulness. Help us to walk the way of righteousness and be productive even as the tree that is planted by the streams of water. Grant O Lord your mercies to us and all the faithful that we may endure the hardships and difficulties that come on us from time to time. Show us a better way. Turn your love toward us in order that we may be sustained by your grace. Equip us for service in the world. Forgive us of our acts of injustice and unrighteousness against our co-workers, neighbors, friends, and relatives. Create in us a clean heart and renew a right spirit in us O God and keep us true to you and your son Jesus Christ. Amen.

God's Glory

Scripture: *Psalms 8: 1*

"O Lord, our God, how majestic is thy name in all the earth."

Meditation

The Psalmist stands in awe of the majesty or glory of God. He praises God for His creation – the heavens, the firmament, and all that is created. Everything is accounted for; moon, stars, sheep, oxen, beast of the field, birds of the air, fish of the sea, and man. The whole cosmos is from God. In the midst of this revelation is man. He is the highest of the created order. He is able to appreciate the creation of God. He has dominion over the works of God and all things are subjected to him. He is given the responsibility of stewardship of God's creation.

Maybe, you too have been able to view the glory of god in the rising and setting of the sun and moon, the twinkling of the star, the babbling of the brook, the rolling of the tide, the meandering, stream in the desert, the chasm of the cliff on the mountain side, or the twittering of the birds in the neighboring tree. The wonders of nature are the wonders of God. An example of this is the Grand Canyon – we stand in awe and cry out "O Lord, our God, how majestic is your name in all the earth."

The barriers of space have been lifted through the impact of science and technology, but they do not find God. The majesty of the being who creates, remains true to the professional scientist and layman. The Lord, our God is majestic. He keeps the world in order. He impresses man with His glory on earth or in space. The mystery remains. But in Jesus Christ, He has made himself known. In the mystery of the Incarnation, He calls us to acceptance of His divine love. We need to see the glory of God in Christ Jesus, our Lord.

Prayer

O Lord our God, how excellent is your name in

all the earth. We bless you for our creation and redemption. You have created us after your image and likeness. You have redeemed us through your son Jesus Christ. You have called us your children. Grant us the courage to be your children. Accept our thanks for the world and all that is therein. Enable us to be good stewards of the riches entrusted to us and by your grace cause us to marvel at your glory in the world and in the cross. Through your redemptive work may all nations and peoples come to acknowledge and serve you through Jesus Christ our Lord. Amen.

The Majesty of God – The Feebleness of Man

Scripture: *Psalms 8: 1-4*
> "O Lord, our Lord. How majestic is thy
> name in all the earth! ...What is man
> that thou art mindful of him, and the son
> of man that thou dost care for him?"

Meditation

In these two expressions there is a striking contrast between God and man. One infinite creator, the other is the finite creation.

The Psalmist opens a hymn of praise with how majestic is the name of God. He praises God for conferring glory upon man. He has appointed man to rule over the entire universe, has crowned man with glory, and honor; has made him a little less than God. He does not sing of praise about man at all. He devotes a hymn of praise about God's majesty in creation. In Psalm 19 there is similar praise given to God and the firmament proclaims his handwork. Even the silent creations of heaven – the sun, the moon, and the stars – proclaim the glory of God.

God has created all things and He will preserve all things. Without God's gift of His spirit, there can be no life upon earth. In God's favor the entire world stands secure and immovable. He is omnipotent (all powerful), omniscient (all wisdom), and immutable (without change or variableness). His power through natural phenomena and disasters does not scare the Psalmist or us. Earthquake, lightening and thunder, hurricane, tornado, flood do not scare us, for God is our refuge and strength, a very present help in trouble.

God reveals himself in nature, in life and death, and in Jesus Christ. He makes known His plan of redemption in Christ. We are called to praise Him for His steadfast love and mercy.

> Praise to the Lord the Almighty, the
> King of creation
> O let all that is in me adore Him
> All that hath life and breath, come with
> praises before Him
> Let the Amen, sound from His people
> again
> Gladly for aye we adore Him.

<u>Prayer</u>

Eternal God, creator, sustainer, Redeemer, accept our thanks and praise for all your love. You have placed us here to be your stewards. Give us hearts and minds to appreciate your handiwork and the beauty of the earth. Enable us to share our endowment with family, neighbors and friends, and to create an environment of praise and thanksgiving. Let the heavens praise you; let the cliffs reverberate with your praise. Let the whole creation rise up in worship and praise to you. Above all, let us fall in reverence and adoration before you this day and always. Amen.

<u>The Lord is My Shepherd</u>

<u>Scripture:</u> *Psalms 23: 1*

> "The Lord is my shepherd, I shall not want."

<u>Meditation</u>

The book of Psalms is the treasure house of Israelite faith and piety. Many of us were brought up on reading the Psalms for family and individual devotions. They give strength and inspiration for the day's work. They sooth, calm us in the evening hours, and act as benedictions for rest and repose during the night hours. In worship, they form a very important part of the liturgy. In sickness, they are the words of hope and Christian fortitude. Before and after surgery, they become the antidote to fear and weakness. In preparation of extreme unction and death, the words of the Psalms (in particular, the shepherds' Psalm 23) are of significant importance. They form the invisible road on which the individual travels in order to inherit the kingdom of God. Think of what it means to say, "the Lord is my shepherd, I lack nothing… Surely, goodness and mercy shall follow me, all the days of my life and I shall dwell in the house of the Lord forever."

The Psalmist summarizes God's goodness as a shepherd. These are the supplier of every need, the protection form evil, the defender of the faithful, the one who establishes His everlasting goodness and mercy, the abiding dwelling place for all the faithful.

Jesus is the good shepherd who provides more than physical and material protection for us. His goodness and mercy can be experienced in His presence in the world. We are called to worship Him where we are;

home, work, recreation. We need the good shepherd in our lives.

Prayer

Lord, we thank you for your goodness and mercy. You have been our shepherd. We are the sheep of your pasture. For your care, protection, and love we offer our praise. Enable us this day by your grace to seek your goodness and mercy. Provide for all who are in need. Grant unto all who work,, a sense of your divine aid and protection. May your love keep us this day. Help us to say with the Psalmist:

> Surely goodness and mercy shall follow me
> And I will dwell in the house of the Lord forever.
> Amen.

The Earth is the Lord's and the Fullness Thereof

Scripture: *Psalms 24: 1-2*

> "The earth is the Lord's and the fullness thereof, the world and those who dwell therein, for he has founded it upon the seas and established it upon the rivers."

Meditation

We are all dependent on "mother" earth. Most of the natural resources are found in the earth. Indeed the earth is the mother of all things. God, the creative spirit, formed this good earth. Wherever we go, we are confronted by the marvels of this earth. It is always rejuvenating itself. While the earth remains, there will be seed time and harvest, cold and heat, summer and winter, day and night shall not cease. This was the underlying covenant with God and Noah and since then all mankind benefits from the covenant.

We live in an age of scientific and technological discoveries. Man has broken the space and sound barrier. We are able to land on the moon and Mars and observe the formation of the planets. The space center on earth traces the movement of astronauts in their explorations. But the Psalmist was not as privileged. In his acknowledgement of God he realizes His supremacy. This Psalm is an enthronement psalm. The chief cantor leads the worshipers in the litany of praise to God.

> "Lift up your heads, O gates
> And be lifted up, O ancient doors
> That the King of glory may come in
>
> Who is the King of glory?
> The Lord strong and mighty
> The Lord mighty in battle
>
>
> Lift up your heads, O gates
> And be lifted up, O ancient doors
> That the King of glory may come in
>
> Who is the King of glory?
> The Lord of hosts
> He is the King of glory."
>
> Psalm 24: 7-10

Like the Psalmist, we stand in awe of the majesty of God. His creation, His mercy, love, and grace. It is our ascription and praise that enables us to wrestle with the goodness of God's earth and bounty. Let us lift up our heads in order that the King of glory may come into our hearts and daily experience.

Prayer

Thou who art immortal, invisible, the all-wise God, we praise you for your creation, both animate and inanimate. You have created all things and given us dominion over them. Grant O Lord that we may truly recognize your goodness in the earth. Great is your faithfulness, morning-by-morning new mercies I see. All I have needed thy hand hath provided. Great is thy faithfulness, Lord unto me. Accept our thanks for your bounty especially your love in the redemption of the world. Grant that we may open our hearts so that Jesus may enter today, that we may lift up our hearts in grateful praise for your redeeming love. Enable us by your grace to ever worship and adore you, for you are great and yet loving and kind to all. Sanctify us by your spirit through Jesus Christ our Lord. Amen.

God is Our Refuge and Strength

Scripture: *Psalms 46: 1, 10-11*

> "God is our refuge and strength, a very present help in trouble…Be still and know that I am God. I am exalted among the nations. I am exalted in the earth. The Lord of hosts is with us. The God of Jacob is our refuge."

Meditation

In the days of Israel's agrarian civilization, cities of refuge were established in the land. These were a shelter for the wounded that escapes his attacker. The judges or adjudicator would intervene and try to settle the grievance. The victim would hold onto the altar and while he is there his pursuer had to await the intervention of the judge.

     The Psalmist regards God (Yahweh) as his refuge and strength. All opposing foes or nations will not prevail against him, "The nations rage, the kingdoms totter, he utters his voice, the earth melts. The Lord of hosts is with us, the God of Jacob is our refuge."
This is a wonderful concept about God. His everlasting love, even from the time of Jacob, will not cease toward us. He will prevail. We only need to be still before Him. Be still and know that I am God.

In a world of strife and animosity whether individual or corporate, we need this stillness before God. He will be exalted in all the earth. The hurly burly of home, factory, office, and other endeavors should not deter us. Be patient and wait upon God, for He is our refuge and strength, a very present help in time of trouble.

<u>Prayer</u>

     Eternal God, you are our creator, refuge, and strength. You are our Redeemer and Savior. You have been faithful to your creation and to us. Be our refuge and strength in these days of stress and strain. May we turn to you for strength each day as we go through life. Teach us to wait patiently for you in whatever we do. Give us the peace that is beyond human understanding. May we rest assured that with you all things are well. Be still my soul, the Lord is on my side. Let these be the comforting words to us this day. And may we be strengthened by your spirit through Jesus Christ our Lord. Amen.

Bless The Lord O My Soul

Scripture: *Psalms 103: 1-2*

>"Bless the Lord, O my soul and all that
>is within me, Bless His Holy name.
>Bless the Lord, O my soul and forget not
>all His benefits."

Meditation

The Psalmist rehearsed in considerable detail
the story of God's saving work in Israel's history. This
is a liturgical psalm, portraying the help of God, given
to a number of groups facing a variety of difficulties.
To each group and individual, God brought succor in
time of distress. He exalts the humble and humbles the
proud. In a personal manner the psalmist recounted the
mercies of God while the congregation and in particular, the choir responded with the refrain:

>1.Bless the Lord, O my soul and all that
>is within me, Bless His Holy name.
>2.Bless the Lord, O my soul and forget
>not all His benefits.
>1.Who forgives all your iniquities, who
>heals all your diseases
>2.Who redeems your life from destruc-
>tion, who crowns your life with steadfast
>love and mercy
>1.Who satisfies you with good things as
>long as you live, so that your youth is
>renewed like the eagle's
>2. Bless the Lord all his hosts, his minis-
>ters that do His will.
>All: Bless the Lord, all His works, in all
>places of his dominion,

Bless the Lord, O my soul.

Examine the ways in which God has blessed you; your home and family, house and property, job and employment, education and vocation, professional training and development, husband, wife, children, parents, friends, companions. These are symbolic of God's blessing in your life. Acknowledge His blessings in your life and continue to praise Him.

Prayer

Our God, who has been our help in times past, and who in your grace and mercy continue to be our help today, accept our gratitude for all your blessings in the natural and physical, educational and social, moral and spiritual dimensions of life. Enable us to offer our thanks and praise to you by service in our homes, at the work place, in the community, the Church, and the nation, in order that your love may reach out to those who are in need. Bless the Lord, O my soul and all that is within me. Bless His Holy name. Amen.

Thanks Be To God

Scripture: *Psalms 107: 1*

"O give thanks unto the Lord, for He is good, for His mercy endures forever."

Meditation

Thanksgiving is a means of expressing ones' appreciation or gratitude for something received or for an act of kindness that has been done by one individual to another.

In all kinds of societies, people have expressed their thanksgiving for the acts of mercy shown by the deity in whom they believe. This is seen in the religion of the Ancient Near East, the Orient, Africa, and in the Ameridian religion, as well as the culture of the Western Hemisphere. Such religious expressions take the form of sacrifice, the presentation of gifts, adoration, praise, and prayer as the worshippers enter into a covenant relationship with the Deity. They seek His protection and promise to serve Him for the ensuing year.

In our Judeo-Christian experience there is the need for thanksgiving. Thanksgiving is an expression to God for His faithfulness in the natural and physical, the moral and aesthetic, and more so, the spiritual manner in which these blessings affect our lives.

Behind all our inventions and discoveries, there is the Divine fullness to which we must address ourselves. We need to thank God for our creation, preservation, and the blessings of this life, but above all for His inestimable love in the Redemption of the world by our Lord Jesus Christ. We need to thank God for personal blessings of health, strength, home, family, husband, wife, children, relatives, friends, intelligence, education, wealth, employment, talents, abilities, the church, and its mission. We need to thank God that we are a part of that mission.

Prayer

> "What shall I render (offer) unto the
> Lord
> For all His benefits toward me
> I will take the cup of salvation, and call
> upon the name of the Lord

> I will pay my vows unto the Lord in the
> midst of all the people
> In the midst of Thee O Jerusalem
> Praise ye the Lord."

Lord, help me to thank you for all your blessings in the past, present, and the future. Strengthen my faith in you in order that I may effectively carry out your command and commission. May your grace be upon all people this day of Thanksgiving. This I ask in the name of Jesus Christ my Lord and Savior. Amen.

The Lord is My Helper

Scripture: *Psalms 121: 1-2*

> "I will lift up my eyes to the hills. From
> whence does my help come? My help
> comes from the Lord who made heaven
> and earth."

Meditation

Psalm 121 is an enthronement psalm. The psalmist celebrates the glories of God's rule as creator and Lord of history. He is a part of history. He has much for which to be grateful as he reflects upon the goodness of god during the past. He intercedes for the continuation of God's loving care in the New Year.

The psalmist praises God even is distress and dejection. The high note of praise is God is my helper. He will keep Israel. He who keeps Israel will neither slumber nor sleep.

> "The Lord will keep you from all evil
> He will keep your life,
> The Lord will keep your going out and
> your coming in from this time
> and forevermore."

Great minds have risen to praise the Almighty God who has taken them throughout their earthly pilgrimage. Some have come from obscurity; others have been richly endowed with this world's goods. In the various disciplines they make their contributions to the ongoing process of life. We think of St. Augustine, Michelangelo, Leonardo daVinci, Einstein, Dewey, Gandhi, and Martin Luther King, Jr. But in the regular walk of life there are people like you and me, who can look back in our lives to someone who shaped our future and destiny. This is our God.

In our world we need to express our trust and confidence in God. Our help is from God who made heaven and earth. Husband, wife, fiancé, an associate, our children, our co-workers, our boss, our colleagues, and ourself all need to recall the help we receive from God. We must look into our lives, look to God. Ask yourself from whence does my help come. You will receive the answer, "My help comes from the Lord who made heaven and earth."

Prayer

God, I thank you for all the blessings you have given me, through the world, family, church, nations, and friends. As creator, you have given me a world with resources. As Redeemer, you have given me your Son to be my Savior. Through your spirit you have sustained me over the years. Help me this day and always to grateful for all your mercies. enable me by your grace to appropriate your goodness in order that I can

be of service to my neighbors, friends, and family. Like
the psalmist, may this be my prayer.

> "My help comes from the Lord,
> Who made heaven and earth".
> Amen.

God's Inescapable Presence

Scripture: *Psalms 139: 7*

> "Whither shall I go from thy spirit or
> whither shall I flee from thy presence?"

Meditation

Throughout the centuries, the concept of God
has been a major concern for man. In the natural as well
as the spiritual order, man has become pre-occupied
with the presence of God. Wherever he turns there is
the presence of God that hounds him.

Creation, history, the prophetic writings, the
word Incarnate, all tell of the revelation of God. In the
natural and physical world God reveals himself. This
can be seen in the rising sun, the moon, the stars, the
rolling hills, the majestic mountains, the reverberating
cliffs, the burning bush, the over arching cloud, the sea,
the dew drop on the blade of grass, all seem to indicate
that there is a sustaining source governing them.

God's presence is universal. His omnipotence,
omniscience, and omnipresence is always arresting. He
is all-powerful, all wise and ever present, and can be
trusted as long as He is God. The psalmist says,

> "Whither shall I go from thy Spirit or
> Whither shall I flee from thy presence

If I ascend to heaven, you art there
If I take the wings of the morning and
dwell in the uttermost parts of the sea
Even there shall thy hand lead me, and
thy right hand shall hold me.
If I say, let only darkness cover me and
the light about me be night
Even the darkness is not dark to Thee
The night is as light as the day, for
darkness
is as light with Thee."

God's inescapable presence can be seen through
a catalogue of events, i.e.: the Garden of Eden in the
cool of the day, Moses and the burning bush, the cross-
ing of the Red Sea, Daniel and the fiery furnace, the
Incarnation, Peter's deliverance from prison, and the
many individuals through whom He has spoken and is
speaking.

In your private and personal life, are you aware
of His presence? Do you ponder the ways in which He
has guided your life, sustained you, and entrusted to
you life in which you can be of service to Him, your
family, your church, and the world? God is in Christ.
He speaks to you. He is always there. In all our actions,
God is present.

Prayer

O Divine Spirit, the Spirit of creation, redemption, and reconciliation, help us to remember you. You
are in our thoughts, actions, and deeds. Enable us to do
the things that are positive and good. May the whole
creation speak to us of your majesty and beauty.
Through the physical, emotional, moral order may we
seek to glorify your name and so appreciate the spiritual
presence that surrounds and fills us.

Touch our lives this day in order that we may worship you in spirit and truth for God is spirit and they that worship Him, must worship Him in spirit and in truth. Amen.

Praise the Lord

Scripture: *Psalms 150*

Meditation

The book of Psalms ends on a note of praise. Psalms 146-150 climax the thanksgiving and praise of the Hebrew people to God for his acts in their salvation.

> "Praise the Lord, Praise God in His sanctuary
> Praise Him in His mighty firmament,
> Praise Him for His mighty deeds
> Praise Him according to His exceeding greatness."
>
> Psalm 150: 1-2

Praise is homage offered as an act of worship, expressed in words or song. Worship and praise has had various forms of expression. There is dance and processional, which prepares the worshippers for expeditions, or induces excitement or anticipation of the divine possession. Instruments are used to intensify the drama and resound with praise.

Musical instruments used in praise are Tom Toms and vocal chants by Africans and Amerindians, wooden drums used by Buddhist; Temple bells in China, India, and Japan. Church bells in Europe and the United States and other English speaking countries, the flute use by the Hopi Indians, the horns used in Greek

Tragedies as well as the stringed instruments used in Hebrew praise. Music and singing constitutes an important aspect of Christian liturgy and praise. Praise is cardinal to worship. It is a rapturous expression of gratitude that follow recognition and anticipation. It recognizes divine beauty, truth, and goodness.

We cannot take God for granted. We are called upon to praise God in His sanctuary. Our lives must show forth the praise of the Almighty God who has brought us to where we are. Let all the people praise Thee O God; Let everything that breathes praise God. We are incorporated in this song of praise. Praise Him according to His excellent greatness.

<u>Prayer</u>

> Praise God from whom all blessings flow
> Praise Him all creatures here below
> Praise Him above, you heavenly Host
> Praise Father, Son, and Holy Ghost.

O Divine Trinity, accept our praise for who you are and what you have done in our lives. The whole of creation joins in praising your name for your excellent greatness and your redeeming grace. Be with all people everywhere this day and grant that in our worship and adoration we may ever praise Thee as the one true God. Amen.

THE HOME STRUCTURE AND FAMILY RELATIONSHIPS

Falling in Love

Scripture: *Genesis 29: 15-20*

> "Then Laban said to Jacob, you are my kinsman. Should you therefore serve me for nothing...so Jacob served seven years for Rachael, and they seemed to him but a few days because of the love he had for her."

Meditation

In the ancient Near East and the Oriental cultures, parents approved the friendship between their daughters and their suitors. They arrange their wedding and give a dowry to the bride. In the case of Jacob, this was not a nuptial, nor an engagement, but approval of friendship between him and Laban's daughter. They were cousins and Laban wanted to keep their "love affair" in the family. Jacob had to earn this by working for seven years.

In our culture, such service is not required. Most young people fall in love, independent of their parents. They make their decisions and later inform the parents. We can learn a lot from Jacob, Laban, and Rachael. It would do us good if we establish a good relationship with the parents of our boyfriend/girlfriend before we embark upon intimacy. To be assured that the parents are in approval of our friendship will prove beneficial to all concerned. We need not "serve for seven years", but allow our friendship to develop as we grow to understand the one we love.

Prayer

Lord God and Father of the human race, we thank you for our creation as male and female and for the sexual and emotional drive with which you have endowed us. Channel these drives through the path of love and understanding in order that we may think and act worthy of our affections and emotions. Lord, we pray for all those who are falling in love; our children, relatives, and friends. Grant them wisdom to choose the right partner in life. Help them to confide in their parents and seek their support in their friendship. Direct them in the path of intimacy and guide them in their love, through Jesus Christ our Lord. Amen.

Engagement

Scripture: *The Song of Solomon 2: 1-4*

> "I am a rose of Sharon, a lily of the valleys. As a lily among brambles, so is my love among maidens…He brought me to the banqueting house and his banner over me was love."

Meditation

The Song of Solomon is attributed to the writings of Solomon and is classified as a part of the Wisdom Literature. Many of us do not agree with the amorous escapades of King Solomon. How then and by what criterion are we to lift up this song to those who are in love and especially to be engaged?

The male consort sees his bride to be as the rose of Sharon and the lily of the valley in all its beauty and grandeur. Beauty is in the eye of the beholder. The fiancé is ready to escort his love into the banqueting house. To be engaged is to be selected and set apart for companionship and covenant. This is the first step in the contract between a male and female who are in love. Hopefully, this first step leads to the second, which is marriage.

The period between engagement and marriage is not only a testing period but also one of mutual trust and consolation. As the relationship develops the couple plan for the day when they will be man and wife. Throughout this courtship they need to seek God's guidance in what they do. Each is a prize to be gained.

Prayer

God, our Father, we thank you for your care over us and for us. You have created us in your image and brought us to this day when we declare to each other our love. Grant that in this engagement, our hearts may become one. Prepare us for fellowship, companionship, and genuine love. Enable us by your grace to esteem each other and live for each other, so that the bond, which you have established between us, may be lasting. Guide us into the necessary preparation for marriage, home, and family. Bless us with your spirit and keep us this day and always, through Jesus Christ our Lord. Amen.

One + One = One...The Sacrament of Marriage

Scripture: *St. Matthew 19: 6*

"So they are no longer two but one."

Meditation

The scripture clearly states that marriage is an indissoluble union. It is a union between man and woman in a life long experience. Many interpretations have been given to marriage. It is for procreation. It is a covenant. It is a sacrament. It is the Holy Estate into which the couple has entered.

People enter marriage according to custom, tradition, and culture. There are many forms of marriage. Some examples are polyandry, polygamy, monogamy, and bigamy. There are also different marriage celebrations. In the Oriental culture, the marriage celebration may last for a week. A dowry accompanies the marriage. The ceremony is held at home, sometimes in a garden or under a tree.

In Western culture, the marriage ceremony was taken over by the church; by the Middle Ages, the Holy Matrimony took place in the sanctuary, sometimes ending in the nuptial mass. The Christian community has celebrated marriage as a holy institution.

Marriage is the foundation for home and family. Two people make a covenant to love one another; to share their lives with one another and to have a family with the hope that God will bless the union. The mystery of love is one + one does not make two in a home but one.

In Genesis 2: 24, "A man shall leave his father and mother and cleave to his wife and they become one flesh." Divorce is not recommended as a remedy for infidelity. "Everyone who divorces his wife except on the ground of unchastity makes her an adulteress, and whoever marries a divorced woman commits adultery." (Matthew 5: 31-32)

Couples are to seek divine wisdom and strength in their marriage. They must have the assurance that God has united them in a covenant with one another and with Him. For this reason they should by prayer and meditation ascertain God's will for their lives, seek the counseling and prayer of the Church, and in commitment to one another and God, enter into the vows that will enable them to out their life-long partnership, realizing that marriage is more than a covenant. It is a Sacrament, a means of grace that permeates their lives and sustains them in their daily pursuits and family living.

Prayer

Dear God, we thank you for the mystery of union of man and woman in the covenant of marriage when two hearts are made one. Bless all those who are married and have families, as well as those who struggle with displeasure in marriage and with their families. Save us from divorce and estrangement. Bind the hearts of husband and wife in love. Help us in our human interactions to remember your love. Be with those who anticipate marriage. Give to them a clear concept of how one plus one can remain one. Strengthen the ties that bind us as a family in order that we may live in love and unity, through Jesus Christ our Lord. Amen.

Mothers

Scripture: *Proverbs 31: 30-31*

> "A woman who fears the Lord is to be praised. Give her the fruit of her hands and let her works praise her in the gates."

Meditation

The last chapter in the book of Proverbs gives a beautiful description of the virtuous woman. She is more precious than jewels, her husband trusts in her she has foresight and vision, she show charity, is brave, industrious, daring, has integrity, is honest, is business like, is a public relations person, is wise, intelligent, kind, hardworking, virtuous, and fears the Lord. The catalogue ends "a woman who fears the Lord is to be praised."

Women have not only been homemakers. They have served in many capacities outside the home. Education has led them into various kinds of leadership. Some examples are politics, teaching, government, medicine, nursing, law, engineering, military, police, sanitation, factory, and the general work force. Many of these are mothers raising their children. They shape the destiny of their children.

On Mother's Day, we honor our mothers. We think of them and the contributions they have made and are making to our well being. The poem by F.A. Campbell illustrates the significance of our mothers:

> Mother, O blessed mother,
> Mother dear, surely is another name for
> love.
> Mother stands for so many things,
> She stands as symbol of love and beauty.
> Mother often times proves herself the
> fastest thinker.
> Mothers are guides to the direction of
> nations.
> Mother is the joy of everything we live
> for,

Mother is the joy of everything we do.
Mother is surely the dearest word there
is
Mother's influence is far and final and
precise.
In our hearts mother is always special
Mother, oh mother, where would we be?
Mother dear, ten little frail fingers
You have reared heroes and valiants and
With God's help guided this mighty
human family.

Prayer

God, we thank you for mothers and their contributions to our lives. You have blessed them with
children. You have provided for them and their families. On this Mothers' Day we honor all mothers. Those
mothers who have predeceased us were good mothers.
Accept our thanks for the teaching and training they
gave to us. Bless the mothers and potential mothers in
our land and the world. Create, O God the environment
of love and service for them in order that they may be
qualified to lead in the home, family, and society. This
we ask in the name of Jesus Christ our Lord. Amen.

The Good Father

Scripture: *St. Luke 15: 31*

"Son, you are always with me, and all
that is mine is yours."

Meditation

Fathers' Day was established to honor fathers. We want them to be assured of their role and importance in the home and family. We give them gifts and send them cards that express our love and sentiments, as well as to let them know how much they have influenced our lives.

The father is a man who begets a child; a male parent, a male ancestor, the founder of a family or race. He is the one who exercised parental care over another. He is a guardian or protector. Father is a respectful way of addressing an old man or a priest. It is the name given to the first person in the Trinity. Jesus taught His disciples to address God as "Our Father who is in heaven, Hallowed be your name." We have come to accept the theology of the Fatherhood of God and the Brotherhood of man.

The Father in the story of the prodigal son shows God's love for His children, but also the Father's love for his two sons. One became a renegade, "was lost and is found, was dead and is alive." The other son remained at home, sheltered, obedient, dutiful, but a remorseful individual. He was unwilling to forgive and forget. The magnanimity of the father is revealed in the son's reception, "Son, you are always with me and all that is mine is yours. Your brother has returned this is where he belongs. Let us make merry and receive him." Such is the role of a good father.

The good father is in charge of his home and family. He is tolerant, forbearing, patient, kind, generous, gracious, caring, and loving to his children and spouse. He takes care of his home and family. He is there to protect, to defend, and to support his family.
His contributions are in the following categories:

1. Economic, where he is the breadwin-
   ner who provides for his home and
   family.
2. Moral, where he teaches values,
   work ethics, honesty, truthfulness,
   integrity, reliability, and dependabil-
   ity.
3. Social, where he teaches the graces
   of living through conduct, etiquette,
   and behavior.
4. Educational, where he shows interest
   in schooling his children, both
   secular and religious education.
5. Leadership, where he is an example
   of trust, responsibility, citizenship,
   and nation building.
6. Spiritual, where he leads his family
   in worship and the fear of God as
   well as in service to God.

The words of this Father's Day card remind us
of the role of the good Father.

May God Bless You Dad
Sometimes it's hard to know what to do
And life seems so difficult and confusing
But always, Dad, you are there for me,
Showing me what is good and right
Helping me make the best decisions
Teaching me by your loving example
And strong, never-ending faith,
And dad, I just wanted you to know
today
How much I admire and respect you,
And how lucky I feel to have a father
Who is such a good and caring man.

Happy Father's Day.

<u>Prayer</u>

God our Father, accept our thanksgiving for
your creation, redemption, and love. You have given us
Fathers that have influenced our lives and families. We
thank you for their contributions and pray that you will
inspire and challenge the fathers of our land to honor
their calling in order that we may have better homes
and a richer quality of life. Let your grace be with us as
we endeavor to fulfill our calling as fathers. May our
children grow to obey and follow your command. This
we ask in the name of Jesus Christ, our Lord. Amen

Home and Family

<u>Scripture:</u> *Ephesians 3; 15*

"I bow my knees before God the Father,
from whom every family in heaven and
earth is named."

<u>Meditation</u>

The significance of home and family can be
seen in the context of love and marriage. We often hear
love and marriage is like the horse and carriage. You
can't have one without the other. So it is with the home
and family, they go together.

The home is the place where love is. A home is
not a house. One buys a house and builds a home. The
ingredients of home are human relationships, interactions, communications, love, and understanding. Fidel-

ity is the hallmark of the home. The home and family is an ancient tradition. From creation to the present, they have existed as an inseparable unit. Civilization revolves around this basic unit with husband and wife as the "given."

The home is the place where the family interacts through love, sharing, giving, peace, happiness, joy, pleasure, sadness, pain, achievements, sickness, death, bereavement, and above all developing the Fear of God. The traditional values still adorn our homes. Home blessings remind us:

> "The crown of the home is godliness,
> The beauty of the home is order
> The glory of the home is hospitality
> The blessing of the home is contentment."

There are many types of families. These are Patriarchal, where the man is the dominant leader or ruler, Matriarchal, the woman is ruler, Nuclear, where there is father, mother, and children through marriage, Extended, family with blood relations such as aunt, uncle, grandparents, cousin, adopted children in foster homes, orphanages, boarding institutions, or children of previous marriage, Single parent, where individuals are either married but separated, divorced, or single, bringing up children. This kind of family is developing rapidly in our contemporary society.

The Family of God.

We all belong to the family of God, whether by creation or redemption. We were all created by God and in Jesus Christ. He has redeemed us. The beauty of the home and family is best seen in the lives of those who acknowledge and serve Christ. For our lives, our homes, and our families to be worthwhile, we must allow God to be supreme in what we do each day.

Prayer

Bless O Lord our homes and families. Grant unto us the necessary provisions for our daily living. Let your blessing be upon my own home, my wife, my husband, children, the families in the neighborhood, and the church family. Help those who are in need of family guidance. Enable us to be teachers, educators, and other worthy examples, in order that we may truly promote the principles and values of the family. Unite us in the bond of love and peace so that we can create true brotherhood at the work place, in our community, and throughout the world. This we ask in the name of Jesus Christ our Lord. Amen.

A Child in the Midst

Scripture: *St. Matthew 18: 2-5*

> "And calling to him a child, he put him in the midst of them...Whoever receives one such child in my name receives me."

Meditation

Everyone was a child. We can all look back on our childhood and recall various things we did, the Sunday school, day school, or the Church we attended. The games we played, the friends we had, the food we ate, our successes, and our failures are a part of our history.

Two centuries ago children were victims of child labor and slavery. They were means of production and consequently deprived of education. Children were to be seen and not heard. They were to be inarticulate. They were like little captives in their environment. Education has removed that silence.

With the changes in education and technology, have come changes in family patterns. Many families have deprived children of their innocence and today, some of our children have become victims of child abuse; children are exposed to drugs, sexual promiscuity, gun crime, disease, homelessness. These are having a devastating effect on the children in our midst.

There are certain characteristics in our children that should remain with them. These are innocence, purity, trust, confidence, openness, irrationality, vulnerability, flexibility, love, a sense of belonging, forgiveness, simplicity, respect for goodness, order, beauty, and humility. The disciples lacked many of these qualities and sought power and authority. Jesus' object lesson with the child in their midst is also for us, "Whoever receives one such child in my name receives me." We need our children; we need Christ in our lives. Let us be humble as we seek and serve Him.

Prayer

> Around the throne of God in heaven
> Thousand of children stand
> Children whose sins are all forgiven,
> A holy, happy band.
> Singing glory, glory, glory,
> Singing glory, glory, glory.

Holy God and Father let your blessing be upon the children of our home, our school, nation, and the world. Let there be peace in our land and love in our homes so that our children can receive physical, emo-

tional, educational, economical and spiritual sustenance
as they develop.

Give us the grace to sustain them in this world
and enable us in our teaching and training to equip them
for leadership in the future. Bless all parents, guardians,
and teachers, of our children. Keep the children ever in
our midst, through Jesus Christ, their exemplar. Amen.

Youth in a Changing World

Scripture: *Ecclesiastes 12: 1*

"Remember also your creator in the days
of your youth."
Meditation

"Youth is what everyone wants, except those
who have it."(Paul S. Johnson, Psychology of Religion.) Why does everyone want youth? Is it because it
seems so radiant and bright with promises or do we
miss it later on and find no way to return to it? Why is it
not desired by all who have it? It is because it is not as
easy as it looks. No age has more perplexing problems
and inner tensions to work out. Youth is impatient for
that which is not yet attained, impatient to explore the
future, to cross frontiers and win a responsible place in
the world.

There are four dimensions of personality development in youth. Personal experiences deepen, social
interest broadens, intellectual powers heighten and
life's purpose lengthens. During these developments,
youth is to remember his/her creator. "The sun and the
light and the moon and the stars are darkened... the
keepers of the house tremble and the strong men are
bent... Those who look through the windows are
dimmed... the doors on the street are shut before the

silver cord is snapped: the golden bowl is broken, and the dust returns to the earth as it was, and the spirit returns to God who gave it." Ecclesiastes 12:2-7

What finality? This is enough to scare anyone into positive response to God and a life of service to church and community. Youth therefore, is the time to serve the Lord. We must teach our young people to serve God now, and grow in grace for tomorrow.

Prayer

Eternal God, you are unchanging. We bless you for your faithfulness through creation, redemption, and the means of grace. We thank you that within your plan of salvation there is no age barrier. We pray for the youths of our land, community, and homes. Grant that through these agencies our youths will be provided for with love and care. Teach them O God to remember you in their educational and social, professional and economical plans. Guide them to the acknowledgement of your love and the acceptance of Jesus Christ as their Savior and Redeemer. In His name we pray. Amen.

FAMILY COMMITMENT

The Birth of a Child

Scripture: *I Samuel 1: 27-28*

> "For this child I prayed, and the Lord
> has granted me my petition which I
> made to Him. Therefore I have lent him
> to the Lord as long as he lives, he is lent
> to the Lord."

Meditation

Hannah was the barren woman. She went to the temple and prayed to God to open her womb so that she could rejoice like all other childbearing mothers. God granted her request. After she weaned Samuel she took him to Eli, the priest and offered him to the service of God. It was for this child she had prayed and now she gives him for the service of the Lord.

This is a gripping and thrilling story. A woman who was barren is able by God's help to have a child and in appreciation for His help she gave him for lifelong service to God. Miracles do not cease. God is able to work for women that are unable to conceive and enable them to rejoice similarly as Hannah. Modern medicine encourages multiple births, but this was not Hannah's prayer. She asked God for a child. Women that are of childbearing age and without a child can ask God to be gracious unto them and He will open their womb.

Prayer

Lord God, Almighty and ever loving Father, we bless you for giving us this child. We thank you for the joy that accompanied the gift. Enable us to nurture, train and care for our child. Grant that he/she may grow in grace and the fear of God. Into your service we offer this child. We pray for all women who are childless. Help them to turn to you and if it is your will, you will grant them the desires of their hearts. Let your Holy Spirit direct our lives, our homes, and our families. May we all reflect on the marvels of your grace in our lives and the lives of our children. Be our God and Savior through Jesus Christ our Lord. Amen.

The Blessing of a Child

Scripture: *St. Mark 10: 13-16*

"And they were bringing children to him that he might touch them… And he took them in his arms and blessed them, laying his hands upon them."

Meditation

The dedication or blessing of children is of historic significance. Parents in grateful acknowledgment to God took their children to the sanctuary to be blessed. God has been gracious to bless their union with a child.

I Samuel 1: 27-28 records Hannah taking Samuel to the temple after he was weaned and offered him to the Lord. "For this child I prayed…therefore I have lent him to the Lord as long as he lives. He is lent to the Lord."

Mary and Joseph took Jesus to the temple and Simeon took him in his arms and blessed God and said, "This child is set for the fall and rising of many in Israel."
(St. Luke 2: 34)

Parents brought their children to Jesus. He dismissed the disciples rebuke and said, "Let the children come to me, do not hinder them for such belongs the kingdom of God." He took them in his arms and blessed them, laying his hands upon them.

From the New Testament times until now, parents have found it necessary to have their children blessed or christened by the church. The ritual is different, but the meaning is the same. God has blessed us with a child. Parents and children need His sustaining grace in their development. Jesus made it clear to us that children are exemplars of the kingdom. There is a special place for them in His kingdom.

Around the throne of God in Heaven, thousands of children stand. Children whose sins are all forgiven a Holy happy band. Singing glory, glory, glory, Singing glory, glory, glory.

Prayer

God our Father, we thank you for giving us our son/daughter. You have been gracious to us in giving us this life to be trained for your service. We are inefficient and unable to fulfill this responsibility without your guidance and instruction. We offer ourselves and this child to you this day and seek your Holy Spirit in his/her daily life. Grant health, strength, protection, physical, moral, and spiritual growth to him/her as the years unfurl. May this child grow to know you and serve you in the name of Jesus Christ our Lord. Amen.

Confirmation

<u>Scripture:</u> *Deuteronomy 6: 4-9*

> "Hear, O Israel, the Lord our Lord God is one Lord...And you shall write them on the door posts of your house and on your gates."

<u>Meditation</u>

The Shemah was cardinal to the religious instructions that were given by the Hebrew parent to their children. It permeated their daily living and citizenship. Religious education begins in the home. Where this is practical (without being extreme and impractical) there is better responsibility to the laws of nature, the laws of the land, and the laws of God.

The Church instructed the new followers of Christ (catechumen) in the words and works of Jesus before they were admitted to church membership. Over the years the Church has seen fit to instruct the young adolescent in the scriptures and teachings. This is called confirmation. Young people are prepared for entry into the body of Christ. At confirmation they declare their faith in Christ and pledge to serve him for the rest of their lives. The Elders and member affirm their faith and pledge their support to the nurturing of these young lives who demonstrate their love for Christ. Confirmation is therefore the gateway into the community of Faith. It is for us to teach, instruct, correct, and pray for our children. As they develop in Christian grace and service.

<u>Prayer</u>

Our God and Father, we thank you that you are

our God and there is no other being to whom we owe allegiance. We thank you for Religious Education in the Church and for its impact on our society and culture. Grant O Lord that all who teaches within your church may be endued by your spirit and equipped to prepare our young people for your kingdom. Bless all who are confirmed. May they be able to discern your spirit in their lives. May their influence be a blessing to their parents, guardians, and friends. In Jesus name we pray. Amen.

Family Illness

Scripture: *St. Mark 5: 23, 40-41*

"My little daughter is at the point of death, come and lay your hands on her... He took the child's father and mother and those who were with him and went in where the child was. Taking her by the hand, he said to her 'Talitha cumi' which means Little girl, I say to you arise."

Meditation

The family is an interesting phenomenon. We share in the joys of birth, the growth and development of the child, the joys of loving and sharing, sickness and sadness, bright days and gloomy days and sometimes death.

The healing of Jairus' daughter is a story of great faith. A father exclaimed, my daughter is at the point of death, come and lay your hands on her. Jesus responded. Like a physician, he entered the room and took the child's hand saying to her "Little girl arise". The twelve year old got up and walked. Jesus told the parents to give her something to eat. This was a miracle and proof that the child was alive.

As parents we share in some dark moments when our children are sick. We also undergo terrible illness. Some of these are determined as cancerous. But we know that Christ was able to heal and raise even those who were dead. He can do the same for us. We need to believe that He is able to do this for us.

Prayer

Lord, you are the Great Physician. You can heal all our sickness and disease. The Bible record reveals your power over these. We pray that you will heal the one we love (mention name) and cause us to rejoice in your mighty work. Increase our faith and bless all the members of the family. Your name is above every other name. We will praise you for your hand in our lives and in our home. Hear our prayer O Lord and grant us your peace. Amen.

You are Your Brother's Keeper

Scripture: *Genesis 4: 9*

> "Then the Lord said to Cain, 'Where is Abel your brother?' He said, 'I do not know; am I my brother's keeper?'"

Meditation

The oldest form of sibling rivalry that resulted in murder is recorded in the book of Genesis. The two characters are Cain and Abel. The tragedy revolves around their vocations and the rite of ancient sacrifice to God. Cain is a farmer, who brought the Lord his offering of the fruit of the ground. Abel was a shepherd

who brought to the Lord his firstling of his flock.
Abel's offering was accepted; Cain's was rejected. Cain
became angry. While in the field his anger developed
and he killed his brother. The Lord inquired of Cain
what had happened to his brother. In deep anger he said
he did not know because he was not his brother's
keeper. As a result of his murder a curse was put on
Cain.

We must note the words of verse 10. "What
have you done? The voice of your brother's blood is
crying to me from the ground." This murder took place
because of the acceptance and non-acceptance of
sacrifice. Fruits and grain do not contain blood. Animal
offering contains blood. The Ancient Hebrew teaching
is the life is in the Blood.

This is true of the one great sacrifice for the
world, Jesus Christ who offers His life for all mankind.
It is in Him that we recognize our brothers and sisters.
We are one family on earth. Our gifts are trivial to the
one Great Gift. It is by the reconciling love of God in
Christ that we become our brother's keeper. We are all
responsible to each other. This accountability creates a
spiritual fellowship. We need this fellowship in order to
stem the tide of hatred, hostility, bigotry, and shame.

Prayer

Dear God and Father of mankind, we thank you
that you are our father. You have given us family with
brothers and sisters by natural birth as well as spiritual
birth. We pray for each one in our family. Bring us
together as brothers and sisters. Remove from us sibling
rivalries and pride, as well as envy and jealousy. Create
in us a clean heart and renew a right spirit in us. Grant
that with the confession of our sins against each other
we may receive forgiveness. Establish we beseech

Thee, the Fatherhood of nations and the brotherhood of man in order that we may come to realize our dependence on your mercy and grace. Heal our personal as well as corporate lives through Jesus Chris who is our one Great Sacrifice. Amen.

PRAYERS OF CHILDREN AND YOUTH

For Grades

Lord, I ask you to help me to pass this test. I need to get good grades in all my tests. If I do not, then I may not be promoted. Lord, I want to be successful. You can help me.

I have studied my lessons, listened to my teacher, and completed my homework. I know that all these preparations will help me, but I am depending on you to guide me in writing my answers. Please do, Lord Jesus. Amen.

In Sickness

Lord, you are my shepherd. You look after your sheep and you will look after me. I am sick and lying in bed, but I know that you are with me. I want to feel your hand on me as I feel my mother's hand on my forehead. Touch me Lord, and heal me. I take my medicine, but I believe you are better than tablets. Heal me Lord so that I can go back to school, play with my friends and enjoy the happiness of my parents, brothers, and sisters. Amen.

In Hospital

Dear Jesus, I learn in Sunday School and from my parents that you heal the sick. I am in this place, which I do not like. I want my parents with me. They come everyday. But this is not my home. I do not see them as often. The nurses and doctors treat me very well, but I want to go home. Please heal me, Jesus and send me to my home. Thank you for all you have done for me. Amen.

Facing Surgery

Father, I come to you, knowing that you are with me. I turn to you as I would turn to my own father. I am to undergo surgery but I fear everything. Take away from me all fear. Let me feel your spirit and I will be all right. Be with the doctors who will operate on me. May all be well with me. In Jesus name I pray. Amen.

Recovery

Dear God, I thank you for being with me in my surgery. You have guided the doctors and nurses. Give comfort to my parents, brothers, and sisters, relatives and friends. Above all you have been with me in the hospital and made my surgery successful. Heal me in these days of recovery and help me to praise Thee through Jesus Christ. Amen.

For Fun

Lord Jesus you were once a child like me. You played with others and had fun. I want to be like you. I want to know how to have fun with my friends without hurting them. We ride bicycles, skip over the tall grass, climb the trees, swim together in the pool, and sometimes go skating, but we sometimes hurt each other. Lord, I do not like this. Help me, so that I can have healthy and clean fun with my friends. Amen.

Holiday

Lord, I wish that everyday was a holiday. I could have so much fun. But then I would not go to school and my learning would be poor.

I thank you that holidays are days for fun and no school. I want to spend my holidays enjoying myself.

Shopping, going to the beach, or visiting my friends. I know I can sleep longer because I am not going to school. Thank you for holidays. Amen.

Travel

Father, I thank you for the world you have made. I thank you for my home and community. There are so many other places for me to know. As I prepare to travel with my parents, I ask you to guide us on our journey.

May these days of travel be relaxing, refreshing, and filled with lots of amusement. Be with all who travel. Open their eyes to the wonders of nature and your love. In Jesus name I pray. Amen

For Parents

Dear God, you have given me mother and father. Bless them in what they do. Let them continue to love me and care for me. I thank you for my parents. I love them and I love you. Amen.

For Brother/Sister

God, I would be lonely without my brother and sister. We laugh and talk, eat and drink, play together and have fun in many other ways. Keep us healthy and strong. Help us to be obedient to our parents and teachers. Be near us each day and moment. Keep us safe. Amen

For Home

Lord, you have given us a lovely home. Mom and Dad have worked hard to provide us with the comforts of our home. Bless them, bless us. Help us to love each other and share in the duties of keeping our home in order. We ask this in Jesus name. Amen.

For Sunday School

Dear Jesus, I thank you for the lessons I learn at
Sunday School. I thank you for the many people that
help to build the church. I thank you for the teachers,
the songs we sing, the acting out of Bible stories, and
the prayer we pray. Bless our Sunday School and may
we all grow to be like you. Amen.

For Food

Dear God, you have given us food to eat. I thank
you for the meat and vegetables, the milk, butter and
cheese as well as the fish and bread. The spices help to
season our food. So many people help me to get food to
eat.

Lord, I thank you for them and pray that you
will keep them well so that they can plant more food for
others and me. Again, I thank you for my mother and
others in the home that prepare my food. Amen.

For Family

I thank you God for giving me a family with
parents, brothers and sisters, grandparents, aunts,
uncles, and cousins. I ask you to bless each one and
help us to love each other. I also thank you for the gifts
they give to me.

Lord, some of us are living in far away places
and do not meet often. I know that you watch over us.
Keep watching Lord. Amen.

For Grandparents

Dear God, I ask you to bless my grandmother
and grandfather. They give me nice gifts and I know

they love me. I love them too and pray that they will live a long time. Give them health and strength. When I visit them let me be of some help to them. Thank you Lord for them. Amen.

For School

Lord, I pray for my school and I pray for myself. I love school because the teachers teach me many good things. You have given us good teachers. Help us to love them and do our work at school. Bless the children in my class. Help us to get good grades and let our school be the best school of all. We pray this in your name. Amen.

For Teachers

Jesus, you are our great teacher, but you have given us good teachers at our school. Much of what they teach us, helps us to good. We need to know more each day.

Lord, bless my own teacher. Help me to show respect for him/her and do the things that are right. Let me be polite. Let me love my teacher. Amen.

For Friend

Jesus, you are my friend, but I have a friend that I can see. We play games and go to the same school and Church. I pray that you will keep us as good friends. Wherever I go help me to remember my friend. Bless his family and mine. I pray in your name. Amen.

First Day of School

Lord, be with me as I leave my home and family for school. I am looking forward to school, but I am nervous and scared. I pray that the children will be nice to me. Help me be nice to them.

I know that school will not be like home. The teaching will not be the same. I would like a nice teacher. I will love and trust my teacher. Jesus, please let me be happy at school. Amen.

Prayer for Graduating

Dear Lord, I thank you for this day. I am graduating. You have been with me all these years. You have helped me to get good grades. My teachers and family were good to me. I am so happy.

I ask you to help me as I go to a new school. I know I can depend on you. Bless all my classmates and friends that are graduating. I hope they will be my friends for a long time.

Bless my mother, father, brother, and sister They have been very good to me. I thank you Lord for everything. Amen.

Entry in College

Lord, here I am in an institution of Higher Education. You have prepared me for this day and have brought me to this place. I do not know what I want to specialize in at this moment, but with your help I think I will know.

I am glad that I have made it to this level and pray that you will give me wisdom and understanding as I deal with the academic environment. Help me to be open to the truth and to use my analytic skill to understand what I am taught.

Be with my parents and family. Keep us strong in faith. May the bond of love keep us, despite the distance that separates us. Help me to respect my Professors. Be with me in all I do. In Jesus name I pray. Amen.

My First Job

Dear God, you are everywhere. I know you are with me. I thank you for my job. Help me to do the work that is entrusted to me with diligence, wisdom, and politeness.

You are the boss and will instruct me how I should do my work. I pray for my director and supervisor that we will be cordial and courteous.

I thank you for my profession. May I use my training for the betterment of this place. Help all of us to responsible workers and citizens. I thank you for the privilege to serve people. Lord, keep me by your grace. Amen.

SPECIAL DAYS

Independence

<u>Scripture:</u> *Psalms 33: 12*

> "Blessed be the nation whose God is the Lord, and the people whom he has chosen as his heritage."

<u>Meditation</u>

All nations and peoples have acknowledged the presence of a divine being. He creates, provides, sustains, and defends His people. As a result, nations and kingdoms have developed. Each of the world's great religions believes in the existence of a Higher source or superior being. They differ in many respects, but propound the theory that an Infinite source of wisdom is responsible for their place on earth as well as their destiny.

The Judeo-Christian religion believes that this ultimate reality comes to us in Revelation. In the Christian religion this revelation is Jesus Christ. He calls us to acknowledge the power of God who guides nations and peoples. Nations and kingdoms have risen and fallen, but the kingdom of God will endure forever.

We are called upon to reflect on the blessings of God on our nation, our people, and in our personal lives. The nation that serves God shall be blessed. The individual that serves God shall be blessed. We all need to turn to the Almighty for guidance, strength, health, and peace in our day.

Prayer

Almighty God, the source of all wisdom and power, yet the loving Father who is willing in Jesus Christ to save us, accept our gratitude for this nation. Bless each individual with your grace, especially do we pray for the rulers of the nation; President, Senators, Members of Congress, Governors, Mayors, and all other public servants. Grant them courage to lead with honesty or purpose as thy serve the nation. Bless each individual in whatever noble cause he/she is engaged and bring us all to serve you through Jesus Christ our Lord. Amen.

Memorial Day

Scripture: *I Thessalonians 2: 13-18*

> "We would not have you ignorant, brethren concerning those who are asleep...For the Lord himself will descend from heaven with a cry of command, with the archangel's call, and with the sound of the trumpet of God. And the dead in Christ will rise first; then we who are alive, who are left, shall be caught up together with them in the clouds to meet the Lord in the air and so shall we always be with the Lord. Therefore comfort one another with these words."

Meditation

Most of us have lost a loved one. Whether killed in battle, died in an accident, was gunned down, committed suicide, died from sickness and disease, from natural causes, or old age. We mourn their passing and remember their place and contributions to life and history.

Those who die in the Lord are with Christ. They rest from their labors and their works do follow them. St. Paul reminds us that, they along with us, will at the end of time join the heavenly host in the presence of our Lord. This is more than consolation. It is Hope.

The Christian religion teaches us that death is not annihilation of the soul. Rather, it is the end of one phase of life and the beginning of another. Eternal life does not end at death. It continues in the hereafter. The soul is conscious in the hereafter, since it will perceive the concourse of those who have been cleansed by the blood of the lamb and clothed in white robes in His presence.

We, the living recall the deeds done by our loved ones. We sometimes feel their presence, dream of them, visit their tombs and attempt to converse with them, thinking they can hear us. We remember our parents, grandparents, spouse, children, brothers and sisters, relatives, and friends who have died. On Memorial Day we honor those who imperil their lives for us. They inspire and challenge us. They have not died in vain. May their souls rest in Peace

Prayer

God of the living, hear us as we offer our thanks for all those who have lived for us and died for us. We thank you for their sacrifice and death; for the deeds of love and for the memory that is sacred to us in that they have nurtured and cared for us in order that we can be of service to our world. Grant O Lord that the challenges of Christian and national service may cause us to offer our talents in creating a better place for people to live. Bless all our families and those who serve at home and abroad. Grant them your peace through Jesus Christ our Lord. Amen.

Labor Day

Scripture: *Ephesians 4: 25-28*

> "Therefore, putting away falsehood…Let the thief no longer steal, but rather let him labor, doing honest work with his hands, so that he may be able to give to those in need."

Meditation

Labor Day originated with Pentecost or the gathering of the harvest. This was when the first wheat crop was harvested. In the British system, this was regarded as Empire Day when the strength of the Empire was made visible through military parades, exercises, and speeches. In the Russian community there is a show of military power in parades and technology. In the American system, Labor Day is the end of summer, recognition of trade unions and celebration of the dignity of hard work.

But in our society there are still inequalities. The "haves" become richer and the "have-nots" become poorer. There is an uneven distribution of wealth, which to its negative extreme leads to unemployment, crime, and its accompanying evils. Many steal from not necessarily the rich, but the poor and aged.

St. Paul admonishes us to work. There is dignity in labor. "Let the thief no longer steal, but rather let him labor doing honest work with his hands, so that me may be able to give to those in need. " This is needed in our society. Each one should put his/her skill to work, developing your God given talent and then we will have not only a better economy but a just, loving, and peaceful nation.

Prayer

O God, the Father of all, you have created man to glorify Thee in the freedom of our service. Pour your blessing upon all engaged in professions, in commerce, in agriculture, in crafts and in all forms of manual labor, especially upon workers in dangerous trades. Grant the skill and progress in knowledge, honesty and faithfulness in labor, and your protection in danger. May there be goodwill and Christian action between all classes, employers and employees, rich and poor, and may all men know their unity is in the great family which is Thine, through Jesus Christ our Lord. Amen.

Reformation Day
The Just Shall Live By Faith

Scripture: *Romans 1: 11-17*

"For I long to see you that I may impart to you some spiritual gift to strengthen you. For in it the righteousness of God is revealed through faith for faith; as it is written 'He who through faith is righteous shall live.'"

Meditation

Justification by faith is a theme in Pauline Theology. Justification is synonymous to righteousness. It is to be free from guilt, to be acquitted by God. Jesus Christ accomplishes this for us. Faith is the essence of things in which we believe. It is abstract and eternal. We can have faith in ourselves, in others, in the church, in God and in Christ. The twin sister of faith is hope.

Martin Luther made St.Paul's statement to the Romans 1: 17 to be the base for his ninety-five these which he nailed to the church door at Wittenberg on October 31, 1517. To Luther and the Reformers, justification is the hallmark of faith in God. Individuals are justified by believing in Jesus Christ who is the Lamb of God that takes away our sins. In our day and age we need to emphasize these facts. If we are to be free from our sins, if we are to justified before God, we need to go the way of the cross and ask Jesus Christ to mediate for us. His sacrifice for us will set us free. We need to believe and then we will begin to live a new life in Christ.

Prayer

Lamb of God who takes away the sin of the world, grant us your peace. Dear God and Father of all, we thank you for sending your son into the world, that whosoever believes on Him shall not perish but have everlasting life. Help us to believe on Him in order that we can obtain justification and live. Accept our thanks for Martin Luther, the Reformation, and Reformers who endeavored to uphold the faith delivered to the Saints. Grant that we may go beyond reformation and seek the transformation that comes from believing your word and living close to you. Forgive us of all our sins and blot our transgression in order that we may enjoy the new life that comes from you through Jesus Christ our Lord. Amen.

Worldwide Communion

Scripture: *Ephesians 4: 1-6*

> "I therefore, a prisoner for the Lord, beg
> you to lead a life worthy of the calling to
> which you have been called...There is
> one body and one spirit just as you were
> called to the one hope that belongs to
> your call; one Lord, one faith, one
> baptism, one God and Father of us all,
> who is above all and through all, and in
> all."

Meditation

The Bible makes reference to the Triune God,
Father, Son, and Holy Spirit. The dogma of the Church
teaches the inseparable Trinity. All who believe
acknowledge the supremacy and unity of the Godhead.
St. Paul explains the new life in Christ to the Church at
Ephesus. Neither Jew nor Gentile had exclusive rights
on the Triune God. God was the God for everyone who
believes.

The churches around the world are observing
worldwide communion day. This is a true application of
the teaching of St. Paul. We are all intrinsically
interwoven as the family of God through Jesus Christ
our Lord. We are called upon to treat each other as
equal in the sight of God, whether by creation or
redemption. The mode of worship and sacrament may
differ, but there is a common denominator that binds us
together as the people of God. This is the Holy Spirit.
There is one body and one spirit that belong to your
call, one Lord, one faith, one baptism, one God and

Father of us all. Such belief eliminates racial prejudices, bigotry and discrimination, geographical and cultural frontiers and unites us as a living fellowship around the world.

Let us be Christian in our actions to each other as we celebrate this oneness in Christ Jesus our Savior and Lord.

Prayer

God, we thank you that there is no division or separation with you. You are one and reveal yourself in one Lord, one Spirit. We thank you for the body of Christ on earth. As the human body is intricately created and able to function in order, even so may your church be united in spirit. Bless all who believe and serve the blessed Trinity. May your spirit empower the Church as a body and individuals to be one and accept each other irrespective of their status in life. May peace and love permeate our lives, our homes, our employment, our community, and our world. Be the channel through which we become one through Jesus Christ, our Lord. Amen.

Election Day

Scripture: *St. John 15: 16-17*

"You did not choose me, but I chose you and appointed you that you should go and bear fruit, and that your fruit should abide, so that whatever you ask the Father in my name, He may give it to you. This I command you to love one another."

Meditation

St. John uses the metaphor of the vine dresser, the vine, and the branches as typifying the relationship between God, His Son Jesus, and the Disciples. A similar unity in function is expected of the followers of Christ, if they are to be productive. "As the branch cannot bear fruit by itself, unless it abides in the vine, neither can you, unless you abide in me."   John 15:4

In our Christian life, Jesus is the one who has chosen us. We are called to follow him. Election is for service and it carries with it responsibility. From the Greek period until now, democracy has been based on the principle of choice. We choose our leaders with the hope that they will serve with sincerity, honesty, and integrity. As we go to the polls to select our leaders we need to ask God's guidance in what we do. We need to select those whom He has chosen. Prayer is the key to this selection. Leaders have abused their privilege, but we can reject those who are unjust, insincere, and misguided in their allegiance.

Prayer

God, our Father, accept our thanks for the unity of the Godhead and for the teachings of scripture. As the parts of the tree are inseparable in their functions, even so may we be attached to you in the production of the fruits of the Spirit. Grant O Lord, that in selecting leaders to lead us in church and state we may be endued with wisdom and understanding. We pray for those we are about to select to govern us. Grant that by thy Spirit we may wisely exercise the franchise, through Jesus Christ our Lord. Amen.

Veteran's Day

<u>Scripture:</u> *I Peter 2: 13-17*

> "Be subject for the Lord's sake to every human institution…Honor all men, love the brotherhood, fear God, honor the emperor."

Meditation

In the first epistle, St. Peter is addressing the members of the Church on how to conduct themselves. He reminded them that they are a chosen race, a royal priesthood. They were no people but now are the people of God. They are to abstain from the passions of the flesh. They are to remain loyal to the human institutions and obey those who are their rulers. They are to honor all men. Love the brotherhood, fear God and honor the emperor. They are citizens of two worlds, the visible and invisible. The invisible takes precedence over the visible .God is the sovereign ruler of the universe.

Many of us have served in wars. Some in World War I, others in World War II, still others in Korean, Vietnam, Panama, and the Gulf War (Operation Desert Storm).
Many have lost their lives leaving their families and nation to mourn their loss. Today we honor the veterans of all wars and thank them for their courage and service to country. They have enabled us to enjoy freedom. May God's blessing be on those who are alive.

Prayer

O Jesus, you are the Prince of Peace. You have called us to be peacemakers with the assurance that the kingdom of heaven will be ours. We come to you in penitence and shame for the loss of lives in the wars in which we have been involved, especially in this century. Forgive our sinfulness and the destruction that we have caused to human lives. We thank you that you have raised up men and women with courage to stand up against aggression and hostility in our time. Bless, we beseech Thee, all our veterans who have imperiled their lives for our sake. Grant peace to our world. May we honor you with our lives. Amen.

OUR MISSION AND MESSAGE

Scripture: *St. Matthew 25: 35-36*

> "I was hungry and you gave me food. I was thirsty and you gave me drink. I was a stranger and you welcomed me. I was naked and you clothed me. I was sick and you visited me. I was in prison and you came to me."

Meditation

What is our mission statement? This question can be raised by the state and government, by the Church, and its affiliates, as well as each individual who realizes his/her mission to society. The church is an agency for the redemption and reconciliation of the world. Throughout history it has demonstrated compassion, love, and service to and for the needy through charitable organizations and missions of various kinds. Barnabas saw the need for helping the unfortunate. He sold his land and gave the proceeds to help the needy. The seven deacons were appointed to care for the daily ministration of the needy and to relieve the Apostles of serving tables.

The Dorcas Society was established to correct the deficiencies of the congregation at Joppa. Paul told the Church at Corinth that God loves a cheerful giver; in response to their charitable contribution to aid his ministry. Individuals have been commissioned by God to help the unfortunate in our society. Denominational efforts, ecumenical structures, and philanthropic donations have established institutions of mercy to help the homeless, the unemployed, the hungry, the prisoners, the naked, the sick, and diseased.

All these efforts seek to alleviate the sufferings of mankind. The church must be a sharing and caring church. Indeed it exists for the sake of the world. Herein lies the gospel. Whether we serve the school, the hospital, the clinic, the food pantry, the store, the nursing home, the homebound or shut-in, the homeless and street people, or those who are behind prison bars the cry of the master will still be heard...

> "I was hungry-you gave me food
> I was thirsty-you gave me drink
> I was a stranger-you welcomed me
> I was naked-you clothed me
> I was sick-you visited me
> I was in prison-you came to me.

This is our ministry. It is spiritual, it is moral, and it is practical. It is love. Everyone can be involved in such a ministry. Will you?

Prayer

Lord we pray like St. Francis of Assisi the prayer of compassion and self-denial. Make me a channel of your love, for it is in giving that we receive, it is dying that we are born to eternal life. Help me this day O God to give my love and service to those who are in need. Help me to show love to the sick, the weak and infirm, the aged and cripple, the homeless and unemployed, the hungry and thirsty, the stranger within my reach, the prisoner behind bars, the frustrated and forlorn, the lonely and desolate, the sinner and unrepentant, that through the means of charity and outreach, I may bring joy to their lives through Jesus Christ who gave his life for us. Amen.

Love is the Key

Scripture: *1 Corinthians 13: 1*

> "If I speak in the tongues of men and of
> angels, but have not love, I am a noisy
> gong or a clanging cymbal."

Meditation

St. Paul in his letter to the Church at Corinth
addressed many of its problems. There was diversity in
the gifts of the spirit. Speaking in tongues was one gift
of the spirit, but it must no be regarded as "the gift".
Those who were endowed with this gift should not laud
it over those to whom it was not given. The fact is the
gifts of the spirit should not cause confusion in the
community of faith. If such a gift is manifest, then for it
to be rightly appropriated, there must be an interpreter
to explain what is being transmitted. The tongues of
men and angels, without love, are like a bell, which has
lost its steel. The sound it makes is not appealing to
heaven and makes a mockery to the one who professes
to claim it as a gift of the spirit. Love is the key to our
witness. Without love, everything we do is hallow.

St. Paul graphically explains what is meant by
love.

> "Love is patient and kind, love is not
> jealous or boastful.
> It is not arrogant, or rude. Love does not
> insist on its own way.
> It is not irritable or resentful .It does not
> rejoice at wrong; but rejoices in the
> right. Love bears all things; believes all
> things, hopes all things, endures all
> things."

196 Lord, Teach Us To Pray

Love is the key to our understanding, communication, and fellowship whether in home, church, or workplace. This passage I Corinthians 13: 4-7 is often used at weddings to exhort the newly wedded couple to practice the ingredients of love in their marriage. But we all need to remind ourselves that the key to spiritual growth is love.

<u>Prayer</u>

God we cannot define love, but we know that you have endowed us with this gift. Help us to seek the love of God, which surpasses all human understanding. In our quest, open the vistas of love to us in order that we may better relate and communicate to our spouse, friend, and acquaintance, as well as fellow members of the faith, and co-workers. Help us to love one another and serve one another. May we seek to serve you who loved the world that you gave us your only begotten Son to die for us. Grant that your love will bind us together as a family and church through Jesus Christ our Lord. Amen.

Christian Freedom

<u>Scripture:</u> *Galatians 5: 1, 13*

> "The freedom of Christ has set us free...you were called to freedom, only do not use your freedom as an opportunity for the flesh, but through love be servants of one another."

<u>Meditation</u>

It is assumed that St. Paul preached to the Galatians during the Second Missionary Journey. A period of three years had elapsed before his second visit to Galatia. During this time divisions arose in the church. The Judaizers (Jewish Christians) wanted the Gentile Christians to conform to the Law of Moses pertaining to circumcision. St. Paul advised the Galatians and the whole Christian community that the freedom of those who are led by the spirit is above the law. The freedom of Christ has set us free.

History has shown that enslavement is wrong. It denies freedom and is the hallmark of injustice and unrighteousness. Many individuals have spoken out against the tyranny of slavery. Some of these reformers or liberators have given their lives for freedom. Such freedom has had political, economical, social, moral, and religious developments. In our modern society we share these freedoms.

> "No man is an island, no man stands alone.
> Each man's joy is joy to me; Each man's grief is my own.
> We need one another, therefore I will defend
> Each man as my brother, each man a my friend."

But freedom goes beyond being gregarious. True freedom is in Christ. We as Christians must move away from sectarianism and seek the Fatherhood of God and brotherhood of man. Surely, our freedom is in Christ who humbled himself on the cross, took upon himself our infirmity and gave His life a ransom for us all. In Christ Jesus, the walls of injustice, oppression, and slavery are broken down and we stand tall as citizens of this world and the world to come.

Prayer

God, our creator, we thank you that all people are created in your image. God our Redeemer, we thank you that your son Jesus Christ has set us free. Enable us by your grace to use our freedom in order to incorporate people everywhere in your love. May we seek to break down the walls of hatred, oppression, and tyranny in the world and create an environment of love and well being among our people. Forgive us of the wrongs we have done against each other and let your spirit set us and keep us free in Jesus Christ. Amen.

The Fruit of the Spirit

Scripture: *Galatians 5: 22-23*

> "But the fruit of the spirit is love, joy, peace, patience, kindness, goodness, faithfulness, and gentleness, and self-control."

Meditation

St. Paul emphasized nine ingredients of the spiritual life. Let me give a definition of each and ask you to draw your own conclusion with respect to their significance in your Christian conduct and living.

Love is the benevolent affection of God for His creatures, or the reverent affection due God from them.
Joy is to rejoice. It involves excitement or pleasurable feeling caused by the acquisition or expectation of good; gladness, pleasure, delight, exhilaration of spirits. It refers to the cause of satisfaction and happiness.
Peace is the state of quiet or tranquility, calm,

quietness or repose, freedom from war or hostility, absence of strife, harmony, and serenity.

Patience is bearing pain or trial without complaining, sustaining afflictions with fortitude, calmness or submission, waiting with calmness, not hasty, long-suffering, persevering.

Kindness is of a good or benevolent nature or disposition. It implies the readiness to benefit or please others as kind actions, kind words, friendly, cordial, pleasant.

Goodness is the state or quality of being good. Goodness implies virtue or integrity, kindness, the best part of a thing, its essence. It refers to the nature of God as being good.

Faithfulness is strict in the performance of duty, unswervingly devoted, loyal to one's promises, trustworthy, adhering to the fact or true to an original. The faithful are the loyal adherents to any party or group. The believing members of the Christian Church of any other religion are known by their faithfulness.

Gentleness reveals kindness or disposition or manner. It is to be mild or moderate as against severe, violent, or loud.

Self-control is the control of oneself or one's actions and feelings. It also implies self-command which prevents the exhibition of emotion.

Now that you have examined these definitions, how do they apply to your living? In what way(s) have we put into practice these thought of St. Paul? How have we treated our friends, our neighbors, and ourselves? If we have failed to live up to the fruit of the spirit, than we must return to God and in contrition of soul ask Him to renew in us the right spirit.

Prayer

Eternal Spirit, the source of our creation and existence, we thank your for your presence in the world and in our lives. Great Father, you have come to us in your son and the Holy Spirit. Descend with all your quickening power and fill our hearts with your love and peace. Accept our gratitude for the work of the Holy Spirit in our lives. We confess that in many ways we have transgressed your holy laws and fallen short of true and faithful service to you. Forgive our sins and heal our waiting souls. Enable us by your grace to put into practice the fruit of the Spirit. May we love one another and above all love you. Strengthen our faith in you and cause us to be of service to our people, our world, this day and always through Jesus Christ our Lord. Amen.